Dear Parent,

Educating your child is one of the most important things you will ever do! But many times, we as parents have difficulty knowing how to teach our children. What techniques should we use? What skills are most important? How much time should we spend each day? **The 30-Minute-A-Day Learning System** is designed to help you answer these questions and to help keep your child learning and growing every day.

Designed by elementary teachers, this series will introduce or review the basic skills for a grade level in simple, easy lessons that your child can understand. In addition, each lesson features an Introduction page to tell you what your child will be learning about, and a unique Review and Assessment page that will help you determine if your child is understanding a concept. These pages also offer suggestions for other activities that will reinforce and expand the skills taught in each section.

By spending just 30 minutes with your child each day, you will give your child an advantage in school and in life.

How to use this book

In order to maximize your child's learning potential, follow these simple steps below as you use your 30-Minute-A-Day Learning System.

- Create a quiet and comfortable work area.
- Gather all necessary materials for the lesson (pencils, markers, crayons, etc.) prior to starting.
- Work only one lesson a day (it should take 30 minutes or less).
- Do the lessons in the order presented. The lessons build on each other; doing them out of order could confuse your child.
- Review each lesson after your child completes it. Determine what areas your child excelled in and which areas need more work.
- Praise success.
- Always help your child correct mistakes in a positive way, as making mistakes is a part of learning.
- The Assessment page at the end of each lesson has a list of other activities that will reinforce or expand the lesson learned by using your child's own environment.

By completing these daily lessons, your child will begin to understand basic concepts. With the additional activities introduced on the Assessment pages, your child will begin to understand how these skills relate to everyday life. By combining these two concepts, you will be preparing your child for success in current and future learning!

Sincerely,

Your friends at Brighter Minds.

Brighter Minds
Children's Publishing™

www.brightermindspublishing.com

Table of Contents

Chapter 1
Language Arts
Letter sequencing 7
Math
Base ten 10
Number words 12
Assessment 13

Chapter 2
Language Arts
Letter sequencing 15
Math
Counting 1-100 17
Number identification greater than 20 18
Assessment 20

Chapter 3
Language Arts
Alphabetizing words 22
Math
Greater than/less than 24
Number value 25
Assessment 27

Chapter 4
Language Arts
Phonics 29
Math
Equal groupings 31
Counting backwards from 30 32
Number order 33
Assessment 34

Chapter 5
Language Arts
Middle sounds 36
Math
Single-digit addition using a number line . . . 39
Number order 40
Assessment 41

Chapter 6
Language Arts
Middle sounds 43
Math
Single-digit subtraction using a number line . 45
Counting Game 46
Adding 47
Assessment 48

Chapter 7
Language Arts
Middle sounds 50
Math
Single-digit addition 53
Adding double numbers 54
Assessment 55

Chapter 8
Language Arts
Middle sounds 57
Math
Number problem 59
Adding three and four numbers 60
Word problems 61
Assessment 62

Chapter 9
Language Arts
Middle sounds 64
Math
Word problems using shapes 66
Money 67
Assessment 69

Chapter 10
Language Arts
Middle sounds 71
Math
Money 73
Assessment 76

Chapter 11
Language Arts
Rhyming 78
Math
Subtracting one to three numbers 81
Assessment 83

Chapter 12
Language Arts
Rhyming 85
Math
Subtracting numbers 1-12 in a problem 88
Assessment 90

Chapter 13
Language Arts
Rhyming 92
Math
Subtracting numbers 1-12 in a problem 94
Word problems 96
Assessment 97

Chapter 14
Language Arts
Rhyming 99
Math
Modeling problems 101
Picture problems 103
Assessment 104

Chapter 15
Language Arts
Rhyming 106
Math
Addition and subtraction symbols 109
Adding and subtracting numbers 1-12 in a
    problem 110
Assessment 111

Chapter 16
Language Arts
Syllables 113
Math
Matching fact families. 116
Assessment 118

Chapter 17
Language Arts
Sight words. 120
Math
Fact families 122
Addition and subtraction. 124
Assessment 125

Chapter 18
Language Arts
Sight words. 127
Math
Illustrating addition and
    subtraction problems 130
Assessment 132

Chapter 19
Language Arts
Sight words. 134
Math
Identifying shapes 136
Assessment 139

Chapter 20
Language Arts
Sight words. 141
Math
Identifying solid shapes 143
Assessment 146

Chapter 21
Language Arts
Word comprehension 148
Sight words. 150
Word meanings. 152
Assessment 153

Chapter 22
Language Arts
Nouns 155
Math
Identifying solid shapes 159
Assessment 160

Chapter 23
Language Arts
Completing sentences. 162
Sight words. 164
Math
Identifying solid shapes 165
Assessment 167

Chapter 24
Language Arts
Capitalization 169
Math
Identifying solid shapes 171
Word problems 172
Assessment 174

Chapter 25
Language Arts
Punctuation. 176

Math
Identifying solid shapes 178
Assessment 181

Chapter 26
Language Arts
Completing sentences. 183
Math
Identifying solid shapes 186
Word problems 187
Assessment 188

Chapter 27
Language Arts
Completing sentences. 190
Math
Identifying solid shapes 194
Assessment 195

Chapter 28
Language Arts
Completing sentences. 197
Math
Identifying solid shapes 200
Assessment 202

Chapter 29
Language Arts
Capitalization 204
Comprehension. 205
Math
Identifying solid shapes 207
Assessment 209

Chapter 30
Language Arts
Nouns 211
Math
Sorting solids. 214
Assessment 217

Chapter 31
Language Arts
Nouns 219
Math
Word problems 222
Assessment 224

Chapter 32
Language Arts
Verbs. 226
Math
Shapes 228
Sorting Solids 229
Word problems 230
Assessment 231

Chapter 33
Language Arts
Verbs. 233
Math
Fractions 235
Word problems 236
Assessment 238

Chapter 34
Language Arts
Verbs. 240
Math
Word problems 243
Assessment 245

Chapter 35

Language Arts
Patterns 247
Verbs 248
Completing sentences 249
Math
Graphing 250
Sequencing 251
Assessment 252

Chapter 36

Language Arts
Comprehension 254
Verbs/Nouns 255
Math
Time by the hour and half hour 257
Assessment 259

Chapter 37

Language Arts
Nouns 261
Completing sentences 262
Math
Time by the half hour 263
Greater than/less than 264
Fractions 265
Assessment 266

Chapter 38

Language Arts
Making predictions 268
Math
Fractions 271
Assessment 273

Chapter 39

Language Arts
Characters and setting of story 275
Main ideas 277
Math
Fractions 279
Assessment 280

Chapter 40

Language Arts
Main ideas of story 282
Math
Patterns using shapes 286
Assessment 287

Chapter 41

Language Arts
Beginning, middle, and ending of a story . . 289
Math
Patterns using shapes 291
Patterns using numbers 293
Assessment 294

Chapter 42

Language Arts
Creating patterns of sound 296
Beginning, middle, and ending of a story . . 297
Assessment 301

Chapter 43

Language Arts
Gathering information from the text 303
Characters 304
Making predictions 305
Math
Understanding directions 306
Graphing 307
Assessment 308

Chapter 44

Language Arts
Comprehension 310
Gathering information from the text 312
Math
Using a number line 313
Assessment 315

Chapter 45

Language Arts
Comprehension 317
Gathering information from the text 318
Math
Understanding directions 320
Assessment 322

Chapter 46

Language Arts
Gathering information from the text 324
Math
Understanding directions 327
Assessment 329

Chapter 47

Language Arts
Gathering information from the text 331
Math
Understanding directions 334
Assessment 336

Chapter 48

Language Arts
Gathering information from the text 338
Characters and setting of a story 340
Math
Understanding directions 341
Assessment 343

Chapter 49

Language Arts
Making predictions 345
Sequence of events 346
Math
Understanding directions 347
Assessment 350

Chapter 50

Language Arts
Sequence of events 352
Beginning, middle, and ending of a story 353
Math
Understanding directions 355
Assessment 357

Answer Key 358
Teacher Biographies 376

Chapter 1

Today's lesson will be lots of fun as we join Marco and his friends swimming in the ocean!

While they explore, you will have a good time learning:
- Letter sequencing
- Base ten
- Number words

Letters in ABC Order

Now make a page for your own alphabet book. Write eight letters in ABC order, starting with **G.** Draw a picture for each letter.

1   2   3   4

5   6   7   8

That's a nice book!

Letters in ABC Order

Color in the parts of the rainbow that have letters in ABC order.

D E F G H

A C B F I

S T U V W

K L M N O

I R L U J

You did it!

Letters in ABC Order

Match the butterfly to the flower that has the next letter.

Singing the alphabet helps you remember ABC order.

Base 10 Blocks (11–20)

Draw the missing blocks to match the number. The first one is done for you.

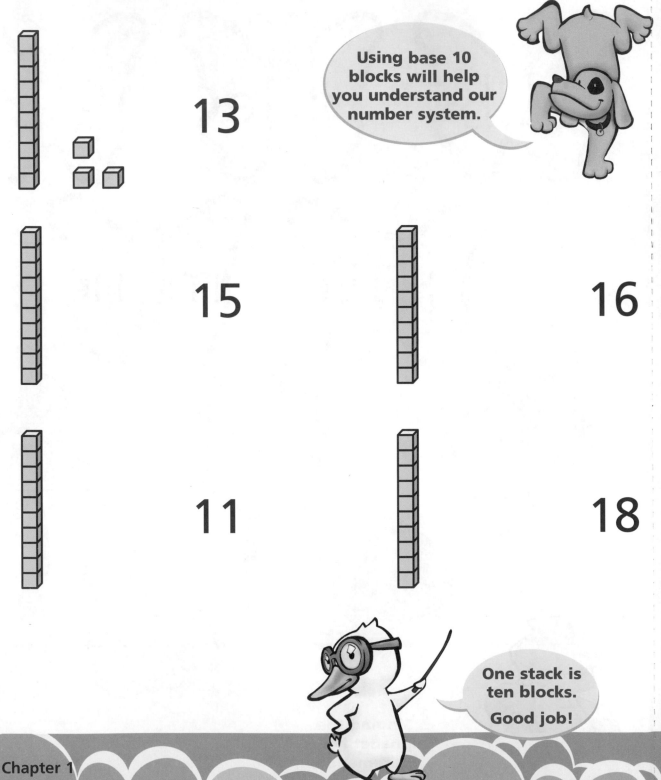

13

Using base 10 blocks will help you understand our number system.

15

16

11

18

One stack is ten blocks.

Good job!

Base 10 Blocks

Color the correct number of blocks to match the number shown under each set of blocks.

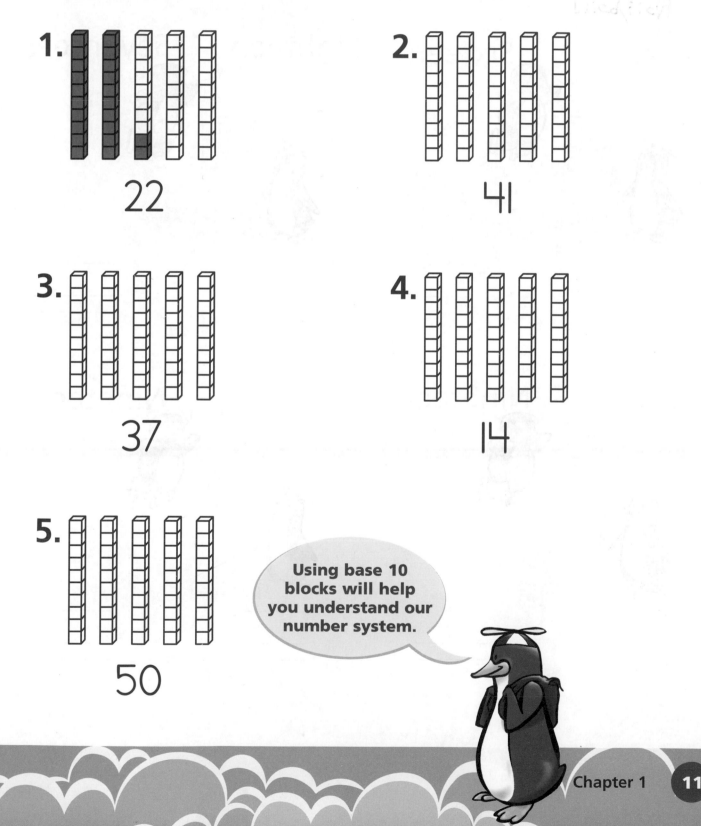

1. 22

2. 41

3. 37

4. 14

5. 50

Using base 10 blocks will help you understand our number system.

Matching Words to Numbers

Write the numbers that show the score of each volleyball game. [Skɔ:]

[Vɔli/bɔil]

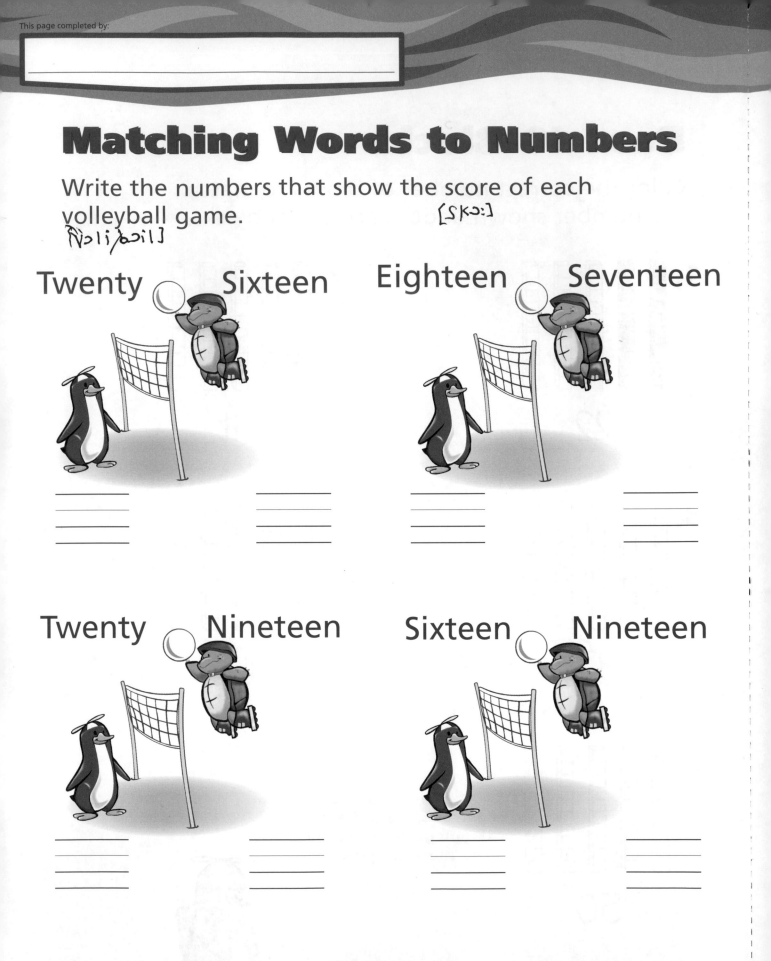

Twenty   Sixteen

Eighteen   Seventeen

Twenty   Nineteen

Sixteen   Nineteen

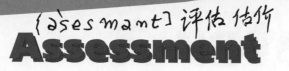

{əsesmənt} 评估 估价
Assessment

Chapter 1 Review

In this chapter, your child studied basic letter and number recognition, as well as base 10 {rekəgnisn} 识别，认识，认出，确认 number identification. {aidentifikeisən} 认出，识别，确认，鉴定.

Your child learned:
- • Alphabetization of letters.
- • Counting of numbers using a base 10 system.
- • Identification of word numbers.

{æktiviti} 活动 活动

To review what your child has learned, do the activities below. Review the pages of this chapter with your child if he or she is having difficulty in any of the areas below. You can also review and reinforce the skills in this section with the additional activities listed below.

{rínfors} 加强 强化 加强.补充

1. Fill in the blanks. a, b, ___, d, e, ___, g, h, ___

2. Color blocks to show tens in order.

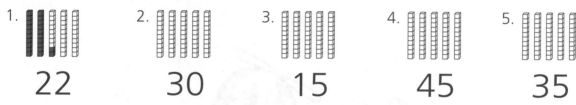

1.	2.	3.	4.	5.
22	30	15	45	35

3. Write numbers 0-20 in order with help from number words.

Zero ____	Five____	Ten____	Fifteen____	Twenty____
One ____	Six____	Eleven____	Sixteen____	
Two____	Seven____	Twelve____	Seventeen__	
Three ____	Eight____	Thirteen___	Eighteen___	
Four____	Nine____	Fourteen___	Nineteen___	

{ədisənl} 附加 补充升级

Additional Activities

Here are some simple and fun things you can do with your child to practice what you have worked on in this chapter. To help reinforce what was learned in this chapter, try these activities.

1. Name a letter and ask your child to guess the next one.
2. Count by tens.
3. Count orally 1-20 while preparing to go somewhere.

to-do 任务 强组

4. Write numbers 1-10 on a to-do list for the day.

{ɔːrəli} 口头的 口述的

Chapter 2

Today's lesson will be lots of fun as we join Paige and Marco flying in the clouds.

While they explore, you will have a good time learning:
- Letter sequencing
- Counting 1-100
- Number identification greater than 50

Now let's see what's going on high in the sky!

Letters in ABC Order

The hats are in ABC order, but some are missing!
Draw a line to show where each missing hat belongs.

Hats off to you!

Letters in ABC Order

Sort the balls. Draw a line from each ball to its correct box.

Counting from 1 to 100

On the beach one night, Paige looked up into the sky and saw many stars. Help her count them. Write the missing numbers in the stars.

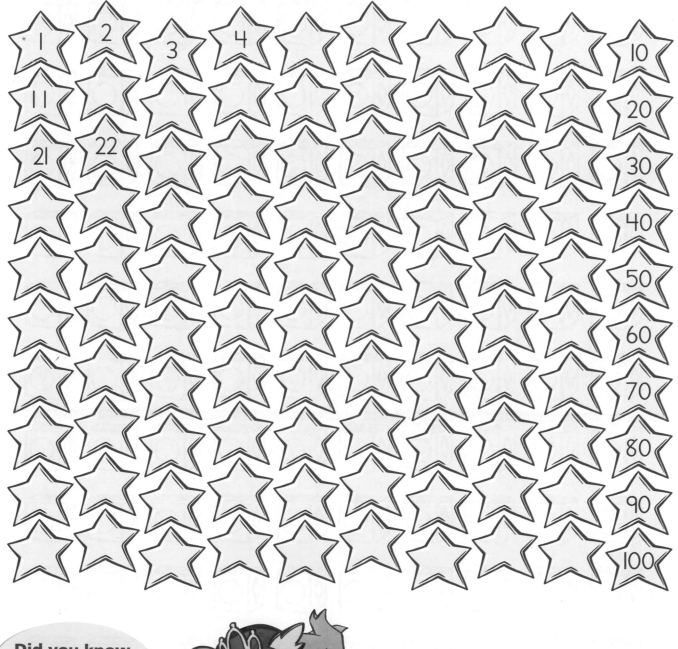

Did you know that you could count so high?

Groups Greater than 20

Color 24 blocks green. Color 35 blocks yellow.
Color 40 blocks blue.

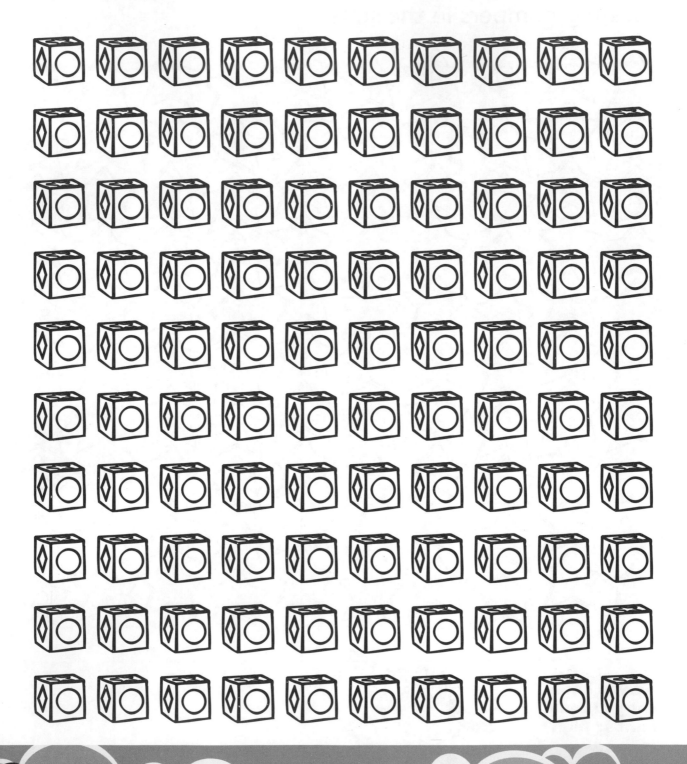

Picturing Things

Help Sam find his way to the toy that has a number less than 50 next to it.

Assessment

Chapter 2 Review

In Chapter 2, your child studied alphabetical order and basic number recognition.

Your child learned:
- Alphabetization of letters.
- Counting and grouping of numbers.

Do the following activities to review what your child has learned. If your child is having difficulty in any of the areas below, go back through the pages of this chapter with your child. You can also review and reinforce the skills in this section with the additional activities listed below.

1. Fill in the blanks with the correct letters:

a, b, c ___, e, f, ___, ___, i, j, k, ___, m, ___, o, ___

2. Fill in the blanks with the correct numbers:

11, 12, ___, 14, 15, 16, ___, ___, 19, ___

3. Circle the three numbers that are less than 30.

11   29   55   2   36   47

Additional Activities
Here are some simple and fun things you can do with your child to practice what you have worked on in this chapter. To help reinforce what was learned in this chapter, try these activities.

1. Have your child orally skip-count by 2's to pick up his or her toys.
2. When your child is in the bathtub, ask him or her to sing the alphabet.
3. With your child, sing "Ring Around the Rosy," but sing numbers instead of the words to the song.

Chapter 3

Today's lesson will be lots of fun as we join Marco and Bogart in the garden!

While they explore, you will have a good time learning:
• Alphabetizing words
• Greater than/less than
• Number value of least to most

Words in ABC Order

Sam can see words in the clouds! Color the clouds in which the words are <u>not</u> in ABC order.

bear
car
daisy

lock
water
tub

house
horn
grass

rain
sun
top

door
eye
flower

net
box
candle

You can see all sorts of things in the clouds!

Words in ABC Order

Color in the ladybugs that have words in ABC order.

fish
gate
house

zoo
yarn
tag

queen
robe
star

ice
jam
kite

rat
sun
log

bat
car
dust

Great!

Which Is Greater?
Which Is Less?

Where there is a number **less** than 50, color the space blue. Where there is a number **greater** than 50, color the space yellow.

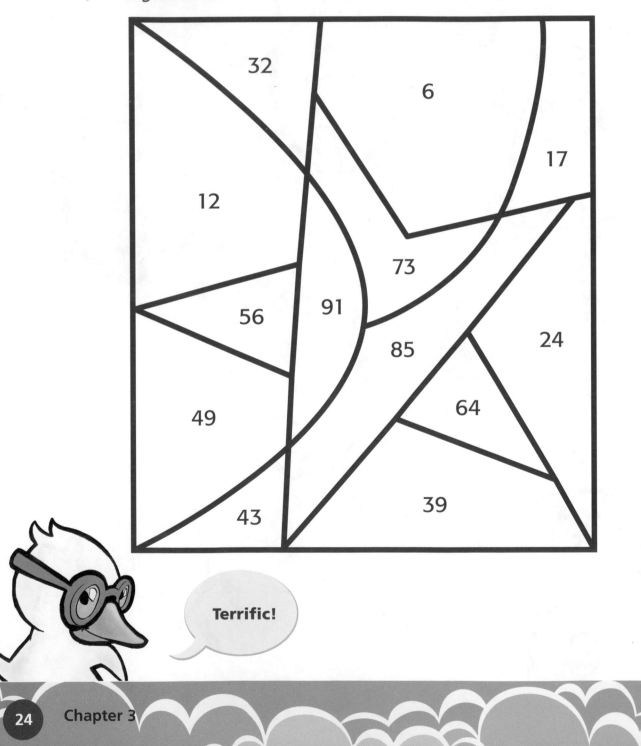

Terrific!

Ordering from Smallest to Largest

Help Quincy build his train tracks.

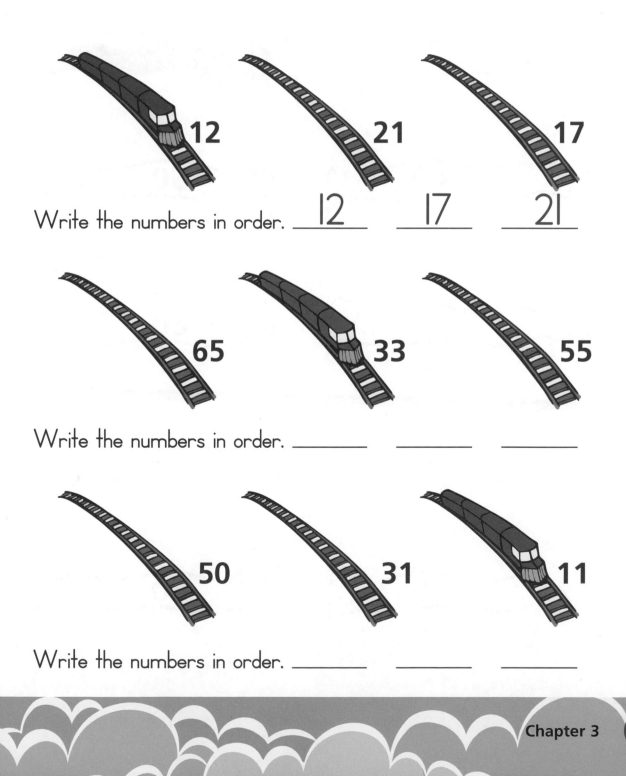

Write the numbers in order. _12_ _17_ _21_

Write the numbers in order. _____ _____ _____

Write the numbers in order. _____ _____ _____

Which Is Closer to a Given Number?

Color the inchworm that has the number on it that is closer to the number shown.

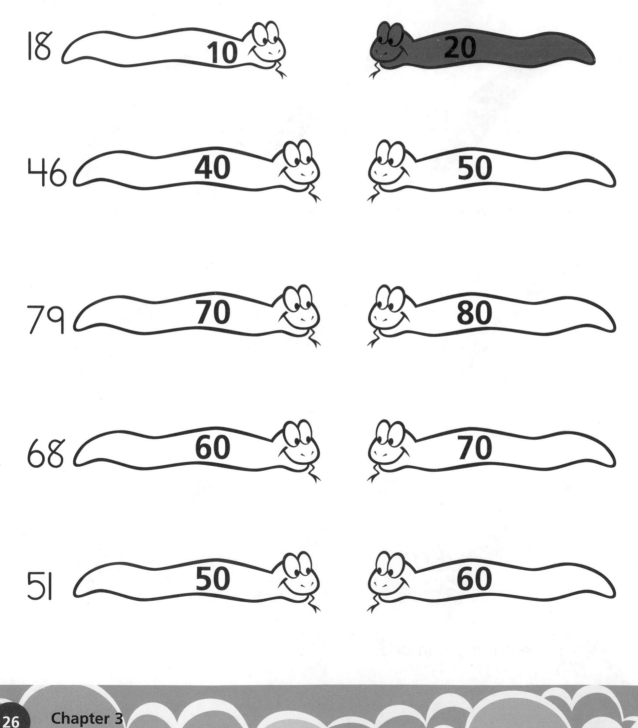

18   10   **20**

46   40   50

79   70   80

68   60   70

51   50   60

Assessment

Chapter 3 Review

In this chapter, your child studied alphabetical order and number recognition.

Your child learned:
- Alphabetization of words.
- Comprehension of numeric values.

To review what your child has learned, do the activities below. Review the pages of this chapter with your child if he or she is having difficulty in any of the areas below. You can also review and reinforce the skills in this section with the additional activities listed below.

1. Have your child put these words in alphabetical order:

flag   dog   cat   elephant

2. Ask your child to put these words in alphabetical order:

on   rat   pear   queen

3. Direct your child to put these numbers in order, smallest to largest:

56   24   71

Additional Activities

Here are some simple and fun activities you can do with your child to practice what you have worked on in Chapter 3. These activities will reinforce the skills your child learned on the previous pages.

1. Have your child write your family members' names on a piece of paper and place them in alphabetical order.
2. With your child, look at a city map. Find three highways in the city. Have your child write down their number names and place them in numerical order.
3. Ask your child to find letters in alphabetical order in the newspaper. Help your child sound out the words he or she finds.

Chapter 4

Today's lesson will be lots of fun as we join Bogart and Sam on safari.

While they explore, you will have a good time learning:
- Phonics
- Equal groupings
- Counting backwards from 30
- Number order

Now let's see what's going on in the jungle!

Number of Sounds

Say each sound in the word **hat.** Circle the beginning sound. Underline the middle sound. Draw a box around the ending sound.

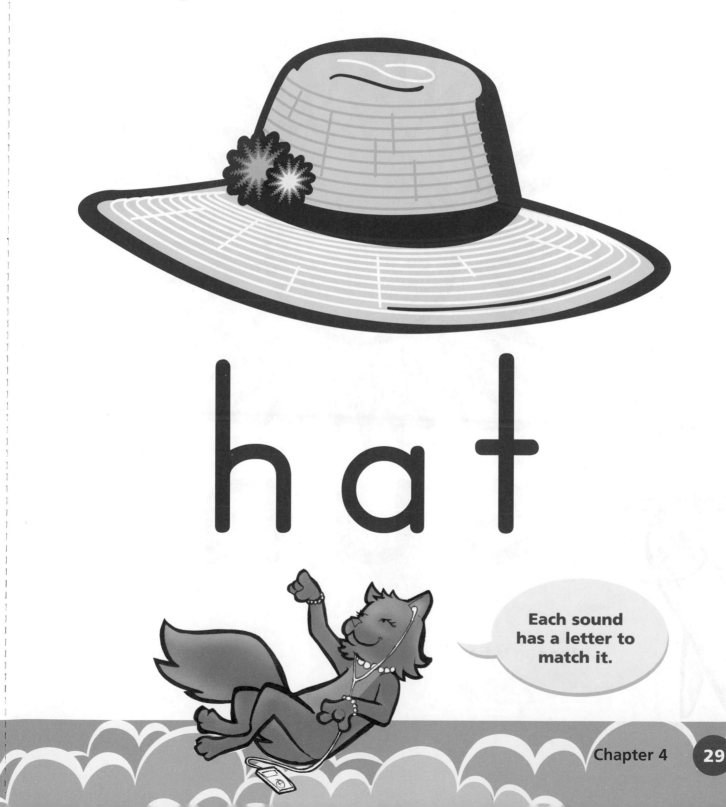

Each sound has a letter to match it.

Number of Sounds

Say each sound in the word **sun.** Circle the beginning sound. Underline the middle sound. Draw a box around the ending sound.

The sun is hot!

Grouping Equally

Draw a circle around the sets of vegetables that will go in the red bag. Draw a box around the sets of vegetables that will go in the blue bag.

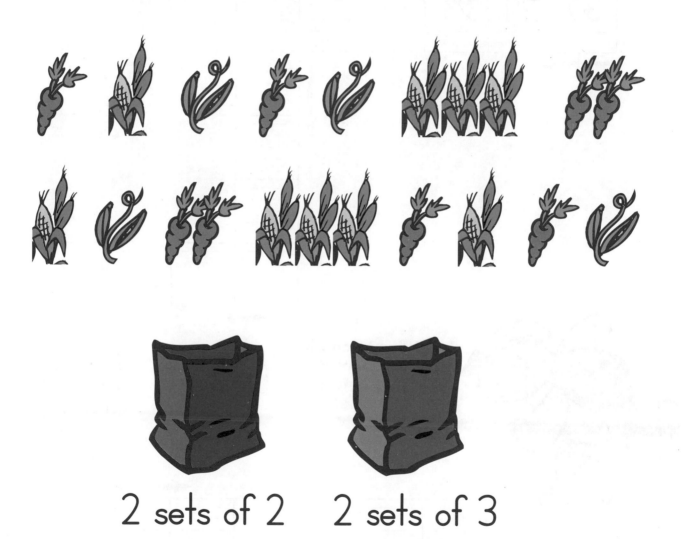

2 sets of 2   2 sets of 3

We have lots of vegetables in our bags!

Counting Backward

Count backward starting at 30. Write each number in the squares.

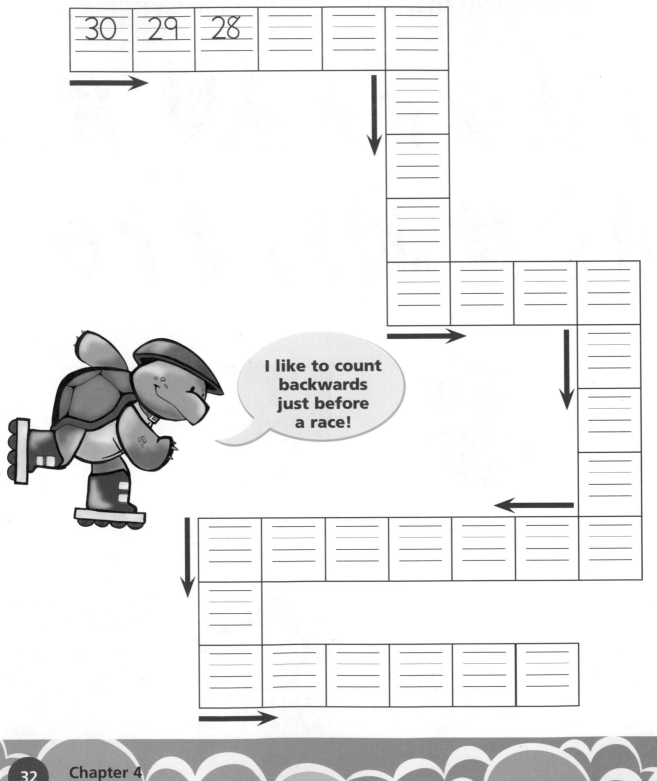

I like to count backwards just before a race!

What Number Comes Before?

Let's go down the slides!

Read the number on each slide. Write the number that comes **before** it.

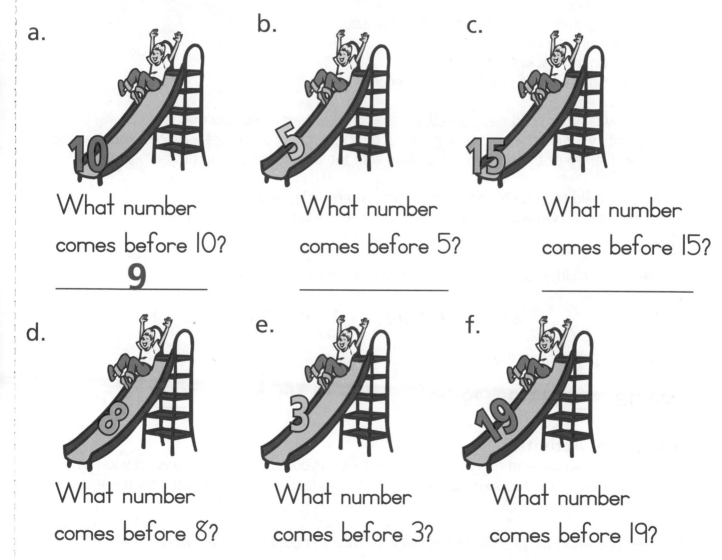

a.

What number comes before 10?

___9___

b.

What number comes before 5?

_____

c.

What number comes before 15?

_____

d.

What number comes before 8?

_____

e.

What number comes before 3?

_____

f.

What number comes before 19?

_____

Assessment

Chapter 4 Review

In this chapter, your child studied beginning/middle/end sounds, sets, counting backward, and identifying numbers in sequence.

Your child learned:
- Recognition of letter sounds in sequence.
- Recognition of sets.
- Counting backwards.
- Identification of numbers in sequence.

To review what your child has learned, do the activities below. Review the pages of this chapter with your child if he or she is having difficulty in any of the areas below. You can also review and reinforce the skills in this section with the additional activities listed below.

1. Ask your child to write his or her first name, then circle the first sound.
   Have your child write a parent's name and circle the last sound.

2. Direct your child to draw the following on a separate sheet of paper:

   2 sets of 4 items   1 set of 3 items

3. Have your child fill in the blanks.

   20, 18, ___, 14   30, 29, 28, ____   5, ___, 3, 2, ___   ___, 15, 14, 13

Additional Activities
Here are some simple and fun things you can do with your child to practice what you have worked on in this chapter. To help reinforce what was learned in this chapter, try these activities.

1. When preparing to go somewhere, tell your child to count to 10 backwards rather than forward.
2. When your child is picking up toys, help him or her group them into sets, such as 3 dolls, 2 trucks, and 6 building blocks.
3. Say a word and let the child identify first and last sounds.

Chapter 5

Today's lesson will be lots of fun as we join Marco and Quincy at the zoo!

While they visit, you will have a good time learning:
- Middle sounds
- Single-digit addition using a number line
- Number order

Now let's see what's going on at the zoo!

Middle Sounds: a

The letter **a** can come in the middle of a word.
In each box, color the picture whose name has
the same middle sound as **cat**.

The middle a
sound you hear
in the word **cat** is
called a **short a**.

Middle Sounds: a

Look on the beach for four things whose names have the same middle sound as **cat.** Circle them.

Can you think of more words with the **short a** sound?

bag

castle

crab

pan

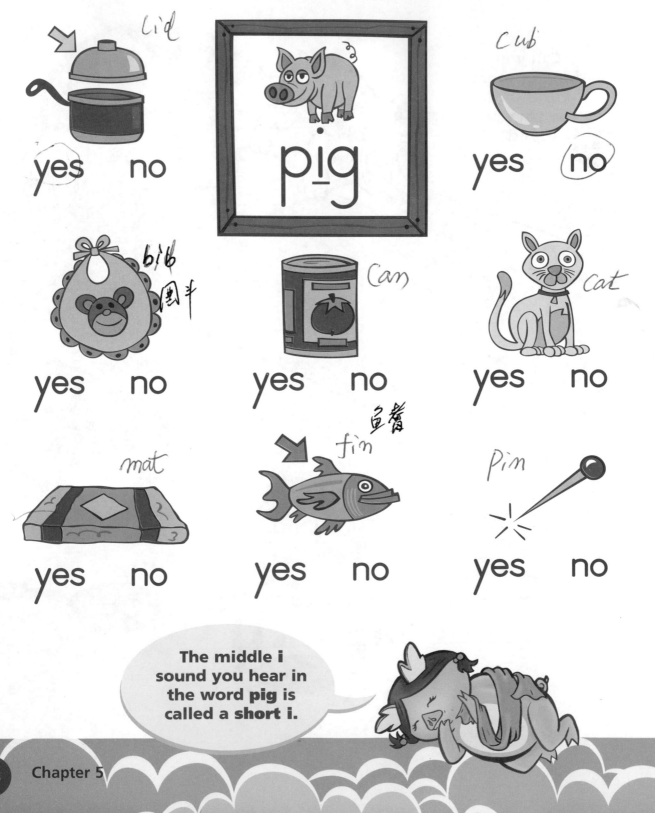

Middle Sounds: i

Say the name of each picture. If the name has the same middle sound as **pig,** circle **yes.** If not, circle **no.**

lid

yes   no

pig

Cub

yes   (no)

bib
圍半

yes   no

Can

yes   no

Cat

yes   no

mat

yes   no

fin
鱼鳖

yes   no

Pin

yes   no

The middle **i**
sound you hear in
the word **pig** is
called a **short i.**

Adding on a Number Line

Use each number line to help you **add.** Complete each number sentence with correct numbers.

frag [frog]

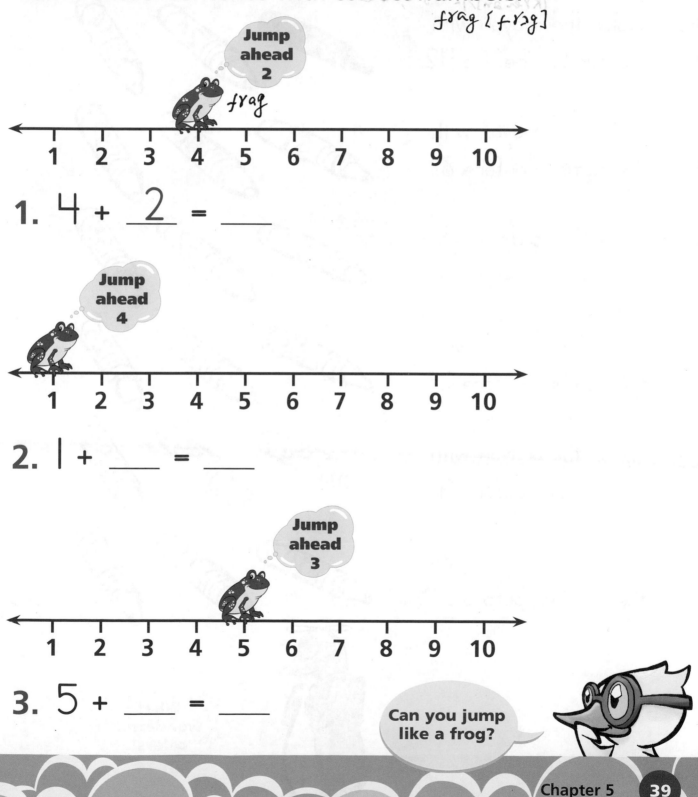

Jump ahead 2

frog

1 2 3 4 5 6 7 8 9 10

1. 4 + __2__ = ____

Jump ahead 4

1 2 3 4 5 6 7 8 9 10

2. 1 + ___ = ___

Jump ahead 3

1 2 3 4 5 6 7 8 9 10

3. 5 + ___ = ___

Can you jump like a frog?

What Number Comes Before?

crayon

[kreian] 彩色粉笔, 蜡笔炭笔

Color the crayon with the number before 42.

Color the crayon with the number before 81.

Color the crayon with the number before 53.

Color the crayon with the number before 27.

Color the crayon with the number before 96.

Color the crayon with the number before 20.

What wonderful colors!

Assessment

Chapter 5 Review

In this chapter, your child studied middle sounds, addition, and identifying numbers in sequence.

[ai'dentifai] 确认.鉴定 于证明
发现.确定
促参与. 使合作

Your child learned:

[rekəg'naizd] 认出, 识别 识论. 承认 认可
* Recognition of median letter sounds "a" and "i."
* Addition by use of a number line.
* Recognition of sequential numbers.

median ['mi:diən] 中位的~中央点 中点

The following activities will provide a review of what your child has learned. If he or she has any difficulty in any of the areas below, go back through the pages of this chapter with your child. You can also review and reinforce the skills in this section with the additional activities listed below.

1. Have your child add a letter to make a word.

bid big bim bit
bad bag ban bat
did dig dim dip
dab dad dam

bi_   ba_   di_   da_

2. On a separate sheet of paper, ask your child to draw a number line of 1-10.
   Tell your child to:

Put your finger on 2, count 3 more = ___   Put your finger on 5, jump 4 more = ___

3. Have your child write the number that comes before.

   23, __   41,____   63,____   19,___   52,_____   89,_____

Additional Activities

Here are some interactive ways you and your child can practice what you have worked on in this chapter. These activities will reinforce the skills your child studied on the previous pages.

1. Help your child think up different words using consonants (B, C, D, F, G, H, J, K, L, M, N, P, Q, R, S, T, V, W, Z) with "a" and "i."
2. Ask your child to use fingers to count up.
3. Use rhyming words to list words with short "a" and "i" sounds.

Chapter 6

Today's lesson will be lots of fun as we join Paige and Sam playing with a ball on the beach!

While they explore, you will have a good time learning:
- Middle sounds
- Single-digit subtraction using a number line

Now let's see what's going on at the beach!

Middle Sounds: i

In each row, cross out the things that do <u>not</u> have the same middle sound as **pig**.

ball

bat

rat

dog

fin

box

milk

apple

Good work!

Middle Sounds: o

Color the pictures that have the same middle sound as **top**.

box

mop

fox

sock

Say the word **top**. Listen for the middle sound.

Subtracting on a Number Line

Use each number line to help you **subtract,** or take away. Complete each number sentence with correct numbers.

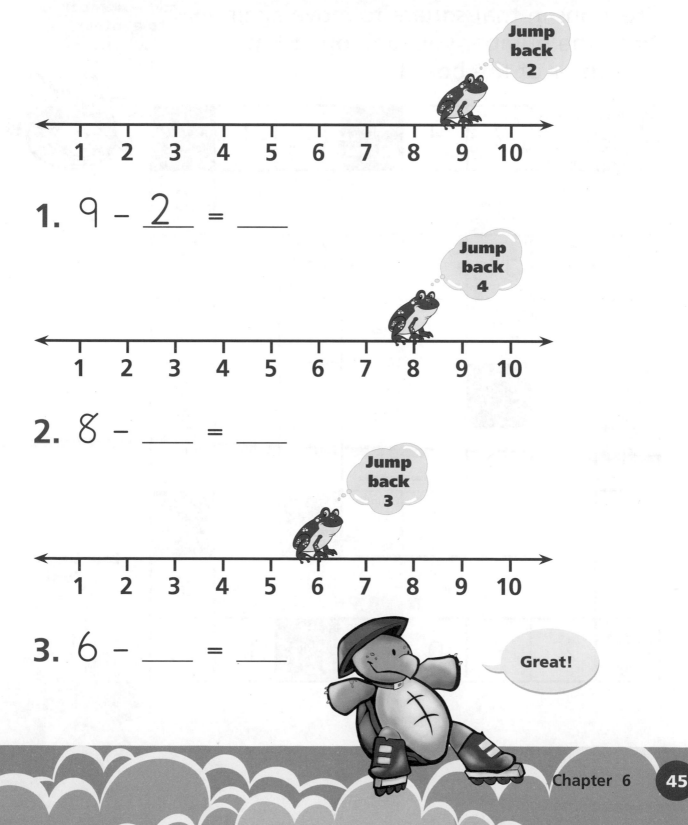

1. 9 – 2 = ___

2. 8 – ___ = ___

3. 6 – ___ = ___

Great!

Counting on to Add 1

Start at 5. Move one square in the direction the arrow points. Follow the directions in that square to move again. Write the number you land on last in the center of the board.

When you count on, you add a number to another number.

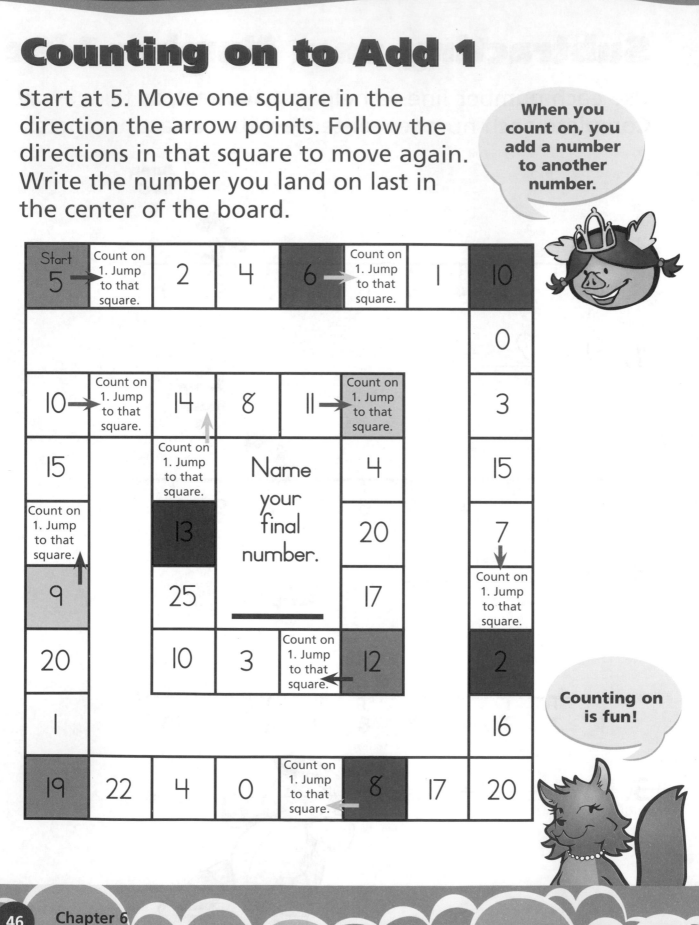

Counting on is fun!

Adding Sums through 12

Help Sam get to the box of carrots. Color each carrot that has a sum of 12 orange.

Remember, a **sum** is the total of the numbers you add together.

6 + 6 = 12	8 + 4 = 12	4 + 4 = 8	3 + 5 = 8
3 + 3 = 6	6 + 3 = 9	5 + 7 = 12	1 + 1 = 2
5 + 3 = 8	0 + 0 = 0	11 + 1 = 12	7 + 2 = 9
7 + 4 = 11	6 + 4 = 10	7 + 5 = 12	10 + 2 = 12
12 + 0 = 12	2 + 10 = 12	3 + 9 = 12	9 + 3 = 12

Thank you for helping me!

Assessment

Chapter 6 Review

In Chapter 6, your child studied recognition of middle sounds, subtraction, and addition.

Your child learned:
- Recognition of median letter sounds "i" and "o."
- Subtraction by use of a number line.
- Addition of sums.

To review what your child has learned, do the activities below. Review the pages of this chapter with your child if he or she is having difficulty in any of the areas below. You can also review and reinforce the skills in this section with the additional activities listed below.

1. Ask your child to fill in a beginning letter to make a word.

$$\text{\_\_ig} \qquad \text{\_\_\_op}$$

2. Have your child fill in the blanks.

$$2 + 3 = \text{\_\_\_} \qquad 5 + 3 = \text{\_\_\_}$$

$$3 + \text{\_\_\_} = 5 \qquad 3 + 5 = \text{\_\_\_}$$

$$5 - 3 = \text{\_\_\_} \qquad 6 + 2 = \text{\_\_\_}$$

$$5 - \text{\_\_\_} = 3 \qquad 2 + 6 = \text{\_\_\_}$$

Additional Activities
Here are some simple and fun things you can do with your child to practice what you have worked on in this chapter. To help reinforce what was learned in this chapter, try these activities.

1. Tell your child to think up rhyming words for:

$$\text{\_ig, \_ip, \_it, \_ot, \_ob}$$

2. Ask your child to sing a favorite song and pick out the rhyming words.
3. In the kitchen, help your child locate some foods that come in groups, such as grapes, carrots, crackers, and eggs. Have your child tell you how many total items there are when he or she adds 2 groups together (such as 15 grapes + 3 crackers = 18). Do similar things to discuss subtraction.

Chapter 7

Today's lesson will be lots of fun as we join Marco and Paige as they visit Marco's hometown!

While they explore, you will have a good time learning:
- Middle sounds
- Single digit addition
- Adding double numbers

Middle Sounds: o

Marco likes to go fishing! Look at this picture for six things that have the same middle sound as **top.** Then circle them.

I hear the **short o sound** in the word **top.** Do you?

sock

clock

jog

box

Middle Sounds: u

Draw lines from the letter **u** to the pictures that have the same middle sound as **bug.**

Say the word **bug.** Listen for the middle sound.

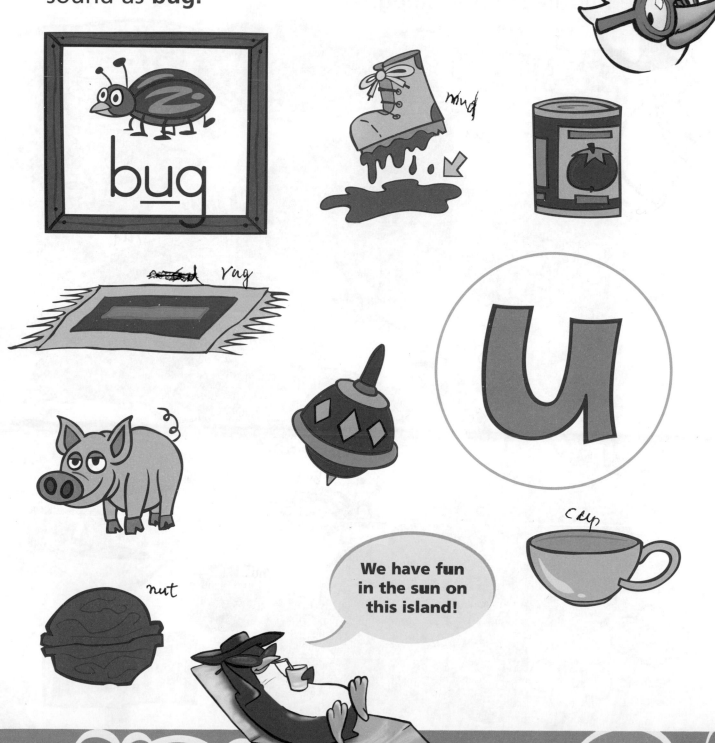

bug

mud

rug

u

pig

nut

We have fun in the sun on this island!

cup

This page completed by:

Middle Sounds: u

Paige visits a beautiful island garden. Help her stay on the main garden path by circling pictures with the same middle sound as **bug**.

Adding Sums through 6

How many animals are in each barn? Count the pigs and write the number. Then count the donkeys and write that number. The **sum** is the total number of animals in the barn. Write the sum to complete each number sentence.

A **sum** is what you get when numbers are added together.

1. __4__ + __2__ = __6__

2. ___ + ___ = ___

3. ___ + ___ = ___

Adding Doubles

Add the doubles next to each dot. Then connect the dots in order from the smallest sum to the largest sum.

When you **add doubles**, you add the same number to itself. Adding 2 + 2 is adding doubles.

$6 + 6 =$ ____

$5 + 5 =$ ____

$0 + 0 =$ ____

$1 + 1 =$ ____

$4 + 4 =$ ____

$2 + 2 =$ ____

I love carrots!

$3 + 3 =$ ____

Assessment

Chapter 7 Review

In this chapter, your child studied the short "o" middle sound, the short "u" middle sound, adding sums through 6, and adding doubles.

Your child learned:
- Recognition of median letter sounds "o" and "u."
- Addition of like numbers.
- Addition of sums.

The following activities will allow your child to review the things studied in this chapter. If your child is having difficulty in any of the areas below, go review the pages of this chapter with your child. You can also review and reinforce the skills covered in this chapter with the additional activities at the bottom of this page.

1. Ask your child to add an ending letter to make a word.

po__   tu__   pu__   ju__   po___   po___

2. Have your child think of rhyming words with short "o "and short "u" sounds.

3. Have your child write the numbers that match the images below.

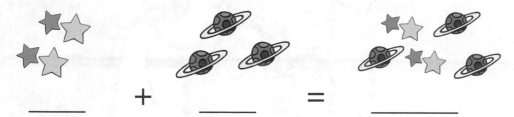

_____   +   _____   =   _____

Additional Activities
Here are some simple and fun things you can do with your child to practice what you have worked on in this chapter. To help reinforce what was learned in this chapter, try these activities.

1. One word at a time, tell your child words that contain the short "o" and "u" sounds (such as hop, rock, pot, and fun, nut, bug) and ask him or her to think of rhyming words.
2. Using pieces of breakfast cereal, have your child count out small groups (of 2, 3, 4, 5, and 6 pieces) and then ask him or her to add different groups together and give you the total. (For example, "3 corn crisps plus 6 corn crisps equals 9 corn crisps.)
3. Ask your child to add numbers aloud to you.

Chapter 8

Today's lesson will be lots of fun as we join Rosa and Quincy investigating a mysterious island!

While they explore, you will have a good time learning:
- Middle sounds
- Number problems
- Adding three and four numbers
- Word problems

Middle Sounds: e

Color each picture that has the same middle sound as **web**.

Say the word **web**. Listen for the middle sound.

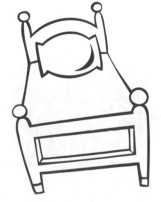

Middle Sounds: e

Circle the pictures that have the same middle sound as **web**.

You're the best!

Good work!

Figuring Things Out

In one monkey family, each 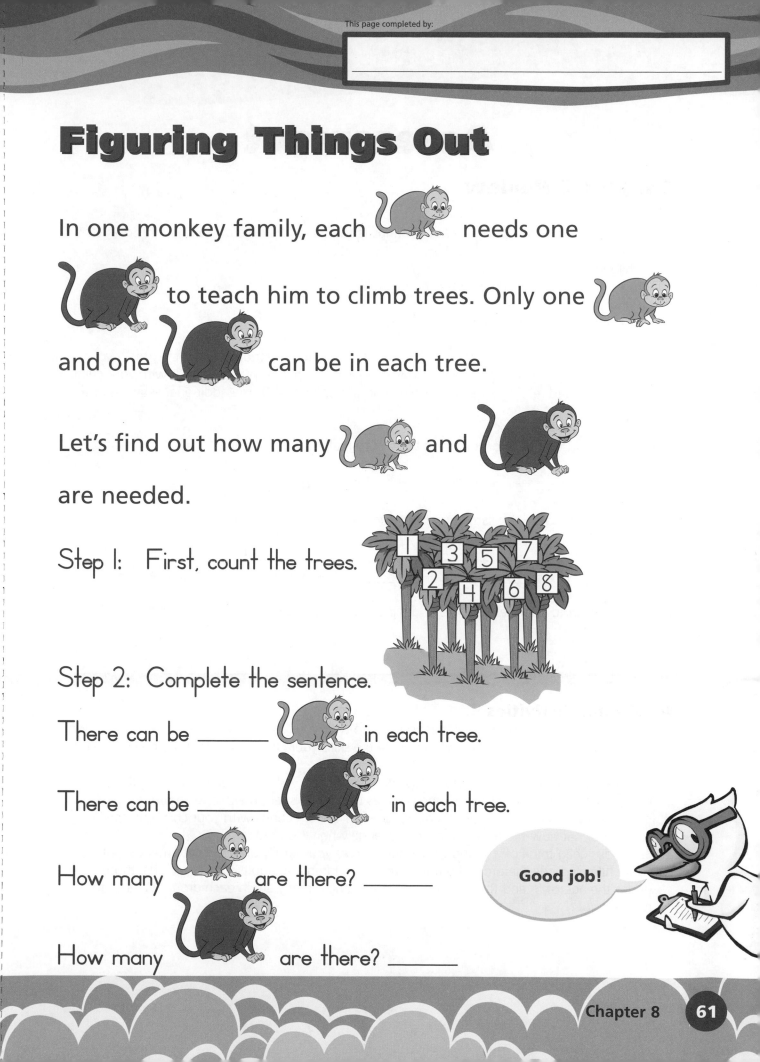 needs one

to teach him to climb trees. Only one

and one can be in each tree.

Let's find out how many and

are needed.

Step 1: First, count the trees.

Step 2: Complete the sentence.

There can be _____ in each tree.

There can be _____ in each tree.

How many are there? _____

How many are there? _____

Good job!

Assessment

Chapter 8 Review

Your child studied recognition of middle sounds, addition, and problem solving in this chapter.

Your child learned:
- Recognition of middle letter sound "e."
- Addition of sums.
- Solving complex problems.

The following activities will allow your child to review the things studied in this chapter. If your child is having difficulty in any of the areas below, go review the pages of this chapter with your child. You can also review and reinforce the skills covered in this chapter with the additional activities at the bottom of this page.

1. Ask your child to add a consonant to the end to make a word.

be___   be__   be___

2. Have your child circle the same numbers, add the two same numbers together, and then add 1.

$$3 + 3 + 1 = \underline{} \qquad 2 + 2 + 1 = \underline{} \qquad 4 + 4 + 1 = \underline{} \qquad 6 + 6 + 1 = \underline{}$$

3. Tell your child to add the numbers underlined first, then add the remaining number to get the total.

$$\underline{2} + \underline{0} + 5 = \underline{} \qquad \underline{4} + \underline{1} + 2 = \underline{} \qquad \underline{1} + \underline{1} + 4 = \underline{} \qquad \underline{3} + \underline{2} + 1 = \underline{}$$

Additional Activities

Here are some simple and fun activities you can do with your child to practice what you have worked on in this chapter. These activities will reinforce the skills your child studied on the previous pages.

1. Go on a "scavenger hunt" in your house with your child. Ask your child to point out things that have the short "e" sound (such as bed, desk, shelf, dress, and so on).
2. Find a recipe in a cookbook or magazine. Go over the directions with your child and then ask him or her how the recipe directions change when it is doubled.
3. Have your child think of a group of people, such as your family or a group of friends. Ask your child to divide the group by traits (such as children and adults, boys and girls, those under the age of 5, and those older) and tell you how many are in each group. What is the total number?

Chapter 9

Today's lesson will be lots of fun as we join Sam in piloting a flying saucer through outer space!

While they explore, you will have a good time learning:
• Middle sounds
• Word problems using shapes
• Money

Now let's see what's going on in deep space!

Same Middle Sounds

Look at the words on the beach umbrellas. Color the umbrellas whose words have the same middle sound.

Nice work!

Same Middle Sounds

Look at the picture. Circle three things whose names have the same middle sound.

boat

bird

fan

bat

Sam

Say the words. Listen for the middle sounds!

Finding Shapes from Their Names

Marco wants to describe the fun he has while traveling in one word. Let's help him say it.

First, circle the letter next to each shape that is named.

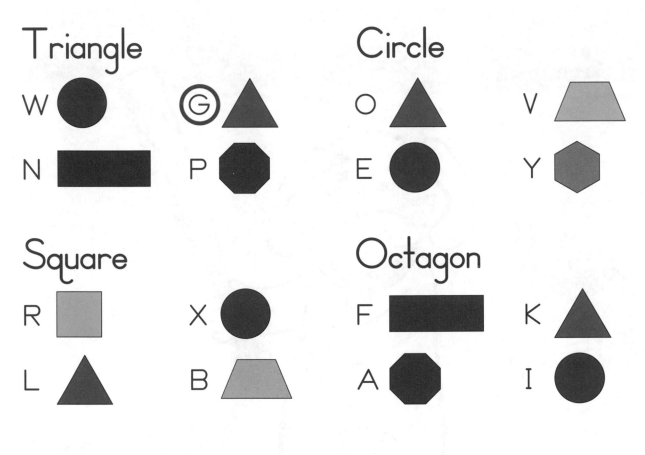

Triangle

W ⬤   Ⓖ ▲

N ▬   P ⬟

Circle

O ▲   V ▱

E ⬤   Y ⬡

Square

R ◼   X ⬤

L ▲   B ▱

Octagon

F ▬   K ▲

A ⬟   I ⬤

Now, in the blanks below, write each letter you circled above its shape.

___ ___ ___ ___ T !
▲   ◼   ⬤   ⬟

Finding the Value of Coins

Draw a line from each group of coins to the tree that shows the coins' value.

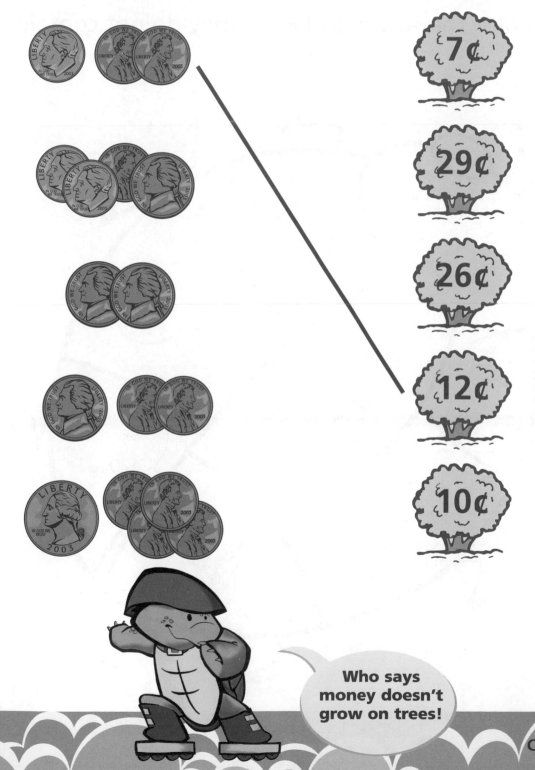

Who says money doesn't grow on trees!

Which Groups of Coins Have More Value?

Color the sections **red** whose value is more than

a 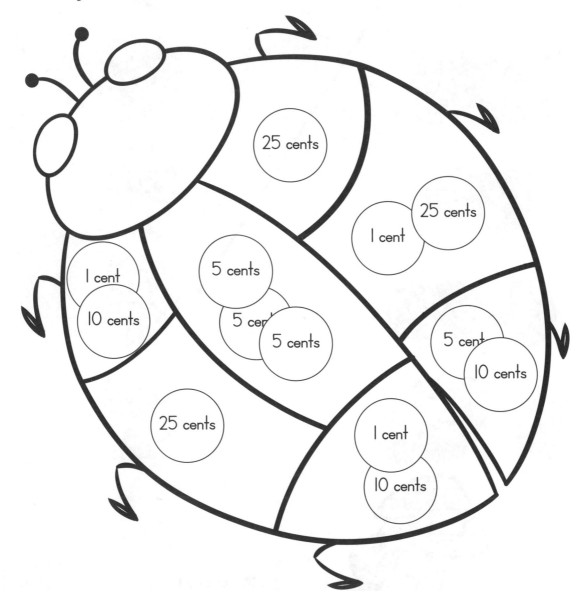. Color the sections **black** if they do not contain

any money.

25 cents

25 cents

1 cent

1 cent

5 cents

10 cents

5 cents

5 cents

5 cents

10 cents

25 cents

1 cent

10 cents

This page completed by:

Assessment

Chapter 9 Review

In this chapter, your child studied sound recognition, recognition of plane shapes, and the value of coins.

Your child learned:
- Phonetic (letter sounds) recognition.
- Identification of two-dimensional shapes.
- Comprehension of the monetary value of coins.

The following activities will provide a review of what your child has learned. If he or she has any difficulty in any of the areas below, go back through the pages of this chapter with your child. You can also review and reinforce the skills in this section with the additional activities listed below.

1. Have your child circle the words that have the same middle sound as HAT.

CAT   MAT   WEB

2. Ask your child to fill in the blanks using the same middle sound to complete each word.

B_ND   S_ND   H_ND

3. Ask your child to think of 3 different combinations of coins that will add up to 25 cents.

Additional Activities

Here are some simple and fun activities you can do with your child to practice what you have worked on in this chapter. These activities will reinforce the skills your child studied on the previous pages.

1. Have your child ask an adult in your family to empty all of the coins out of his or her pocket or purse and count them.
2. When you're traveling in a car, have your child identify the shapes of road signs.
3. Say two words to your child and then ask if they have the same middle sound.

Chapter 10

Today's lesson will be lots of fun as we join Quincy and Sam at the zoo!

While they explore, you will have a good time learning:
• Middle sounds
• Money

Now let's see what's going on at the zoo!

Same Middle Sounds

Quincy wants to get an ice cream cone! Help him find his way to the ice cream truck. Connect the words that share the same middle sound.

book

hat

START

net

ten **10**

hen

pig

web

pot

Same Middle Sounds

Help Sam pack his beach bags. Things with names that have an **o** middle sound go in the **o** bag. Things with names that have an **i** middle sound go in the **i** bag.

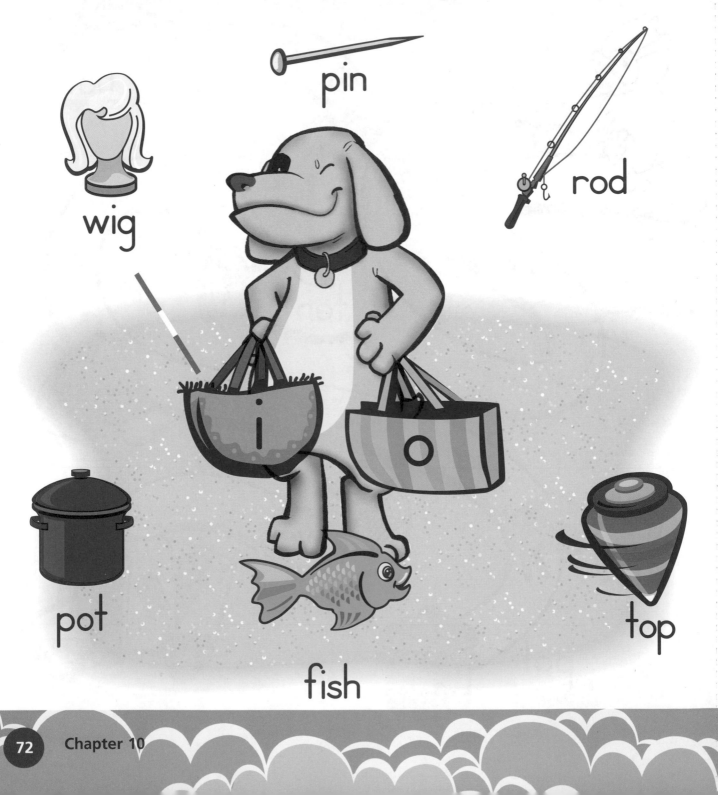

pin

wig

rod

pot

fish

top

Matching Groups of Coins

Color the groups of coins that equal 10¢ red.
Color the groups of coins that equal 30¢ blue.
Color the groups of coins that equal 50¢ green.

If two or more coins are of equal value, then all are worth the same amount.

Which Group of Coins Has Less Value?

For each group, circle the amount of money that is **less**.

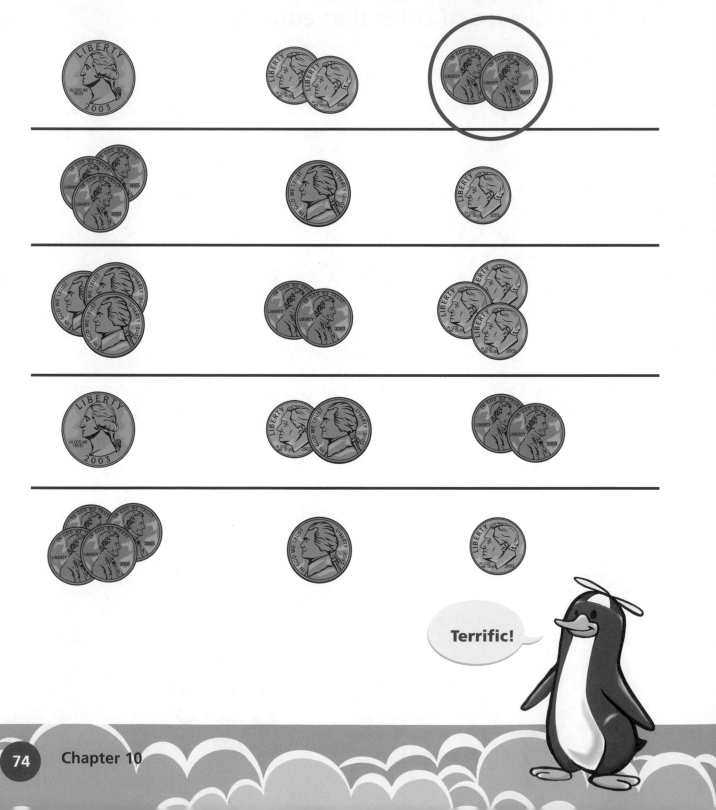

Terrific!

Talking About Things

You want to buy some seeds for a garden but you don't have any money. Ask three people to each lend you five coins.

If someone gave you two dimes and three pennies, you would have 23 cents.

Name _____

How many coins? _____

Draw the coins.

What is their value? _____

Name _____

How many coins? _____

Draw the coins.

What is their value? _____

Name _____

How many coins? _____

Draw the coins.

How many coins did you collect?

What is their value? _____

Assessment

Chapter 10 Review

In this chapter, your child studied similar middle sounds and coin values.

Your child learned:
- Phonetic (letter sounds) recognition.
- Comprehension of the monetary value of coins.

To review what your child has learned, do the 3 activities below. If your child is having difficulty in any of the areas below, go back and review the pages with him or her. You can also review and reinforce the skills in this section with the additional activities listed below.

1. Ask your child to sort these words by similar middle sounds:

TUB   BUG   HAT
BAT   RUG   CAT

2. Have your child add the following combinations of coins.

Dime + Dime + Dime = _____
Dime + Dime + Nickel = _____
Quarter + Nickel + Dime = _____

3. Instruct your child to draw a line connecting words with the same middle sounds:

PIG   TEN
HEN   WIG
POT   HOT

Additional Activities

Below are some interactive ways you and your child can review what you have worked on in this chapter. These activities will reinforce the skills your child studied on the previous pages.

1. Have your child empty their piggy bank, or give them your loose change, then ask them to sort them by type of coin.
2. After your child sorts the change from the above activity, ask them which coin they have the most/least of.
3. Ask your child to name as many words as they can that have the same middle sound as TOP.

Chapter 11

Today's lesson will be lots of fun as we join Marco while he slides down the snow on his belly!

While he slides, you will have a good time learning:
- Rhyming
- Subtracting one to three numbers

Now let's see what's happening in the snow!

Rhyming Words

A cave explorer comes along. He has a net with him. Help the explorer find Sam in the cave. Draw lines between the words that rhyme with **net.**

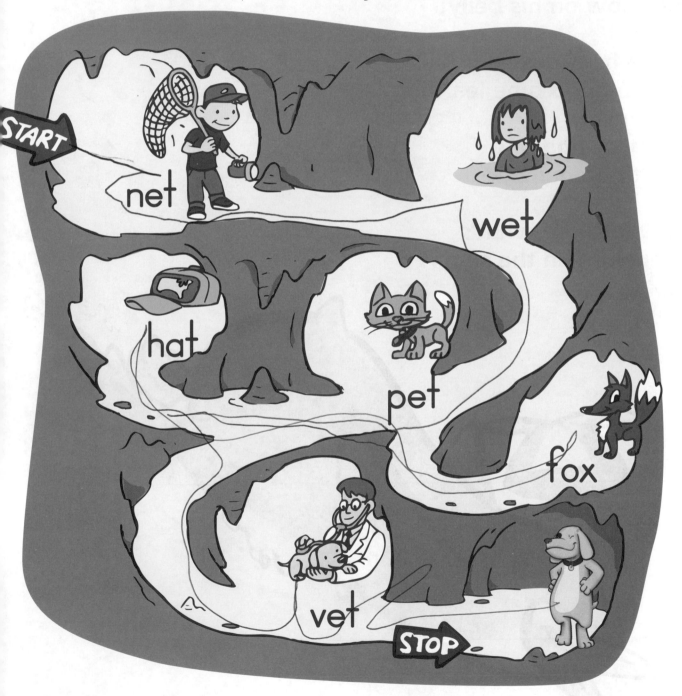

Rhyming Words

Quincy finds some old cups in the dim cave. They have names on them! Draw lines from the word **dim** to each name that rhymes with it.

dim

Kim

Sam

Pat

Tim

Jim

Jen

Remember, words that rhyme have the same middle and ending sounds.

Rhyming Words

Say each word below. Match the words that rhyme.

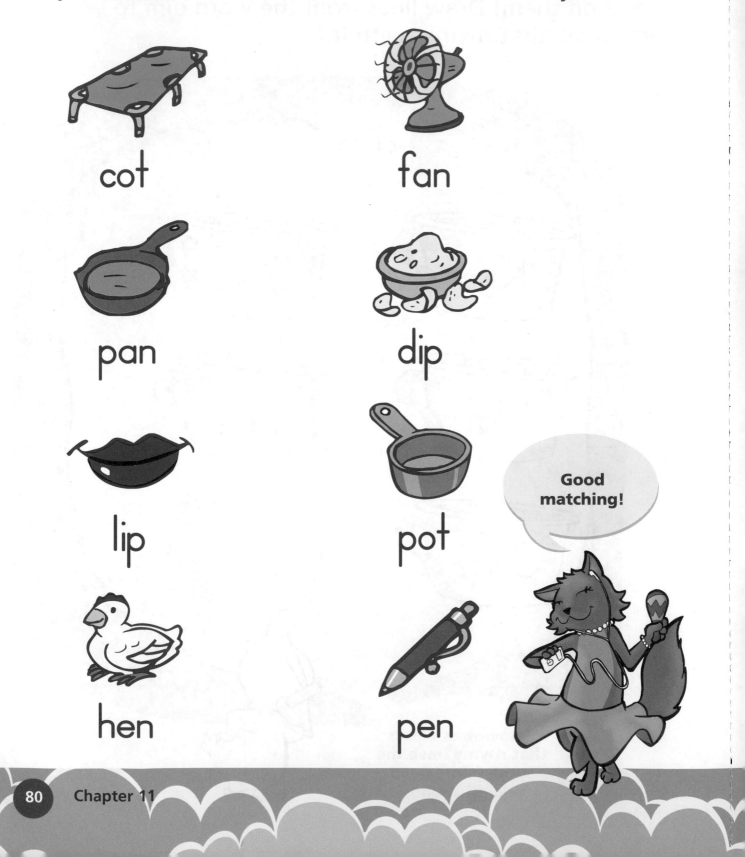

cot

fan

pan

dip

lip

pot

Good matching!

hen

pen

Counting back to Subtract 1

Count back from each apple on the tree by one. Then draw a line from each apple on the tree to the apple on the ground that shows one less than that number.

When you **count back**, you subtract or take away from each number.

You are good at subtracting!

Subtracting with Numbers 1 through 3

Draw an *X* over each falling apple. **Subtract** the apples that are falling from the total number of apples. Complete each number sentence.

Remember, to subtract means to take away.

1. _____ - _____ = _____

2. _____ - _____ = _____

Seeing all those apples makes me hungry!

3. _____ - _____ = _____

Assessment

Chapter 11

In this chapter, your child studied similar sounding words, counting back, and subtracting numbers 1 through 3.

Your child learned:
- Phonetic (letter sounds) recognition.
- Subtraction.
- Identification of rhyming words.

Work with your child on the chapter review activities shown below. If your child has difficulty with any of these exercises, go back through the chapter with him or her to review the material. You can also review and reinforce these skills with your child using the exercises in the additional activities section below.

1. Have your child write the number that comes before.

__ ,8   __ ,10   __ ,13   __ ,16   __ ,19

2. Circle the words that rhyme with SING.

RING	BALL	PING
SAT	STRING	SANG

3. Have your child fill in the blanks.

5 – 3 = ___   6 – 2 = ___
3 – 1 = ___   4 – 1 = ___

Additional Activities

Below are some interactive ways you and your child can practice what you have worked on in this chapter. These activities will reinforce the skills your child studied on the previous pages.

1. Teach your child your favorite nursery rhyme.
2. Have your child say a word and see who comes up with the most words that rhyme with that word.
3. Give your child 10 pennies. Ask your child how many pennies they would have to take away from the pile so that there are only 5 left.

Chapter 12

Today's lesson will be lots of fun as we join Marco and Bogart while they splash in the pool!

(splⁿʃ) 濺、潑.激起水花

While they explore, you will have a good time learning:
- Rhyming [ˈrai miŋ] 押韵
- Subtracting numbers 1-12 in a problem

Now let's see what's going on in the pool!

Rhyming Words

Read each pair of words below. If they rhyme, circle the picture.

fat cat

pet kit

pûp cûp

red bed

sad lad

hot sun

That lad really looks sad!

Rhyming Words

Write each word in the box next to the word it rhymes with below.

man	pot	net	lid

dot _____

wet _____

fan _____

hid _____

Can you think of more words that rhyme with each word above?

Rhyming Words

A pig wanders into the cave!
Circle the words that rhyme with **pig**.

sit

jig

dig

run

pig

wig

Say the word **pig**
out loud. What middle
and ending sounds
do you hear?

Subtracting Numbers through 6

In each group of animals, circle the animals that do not belong on the farm. Then **subtract** the animals that do not belong on the farm from the total number of animals. Complete each number sentence.

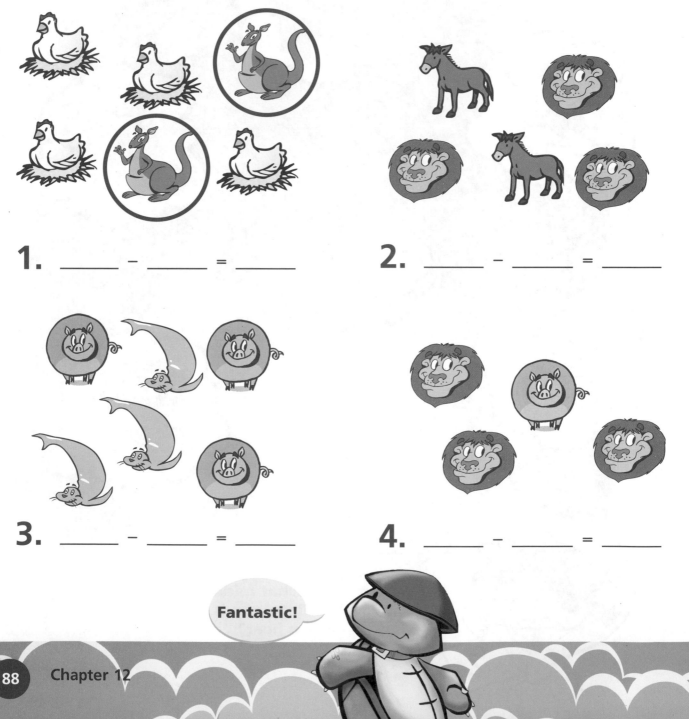

1. _____ – _____ = _____

2. _____ – _____ = _____

3. _____ – _____ = _____

4. _____ – _____ = _____

Fantastic!

Subtracting Numbers through 12

Vegetables are a common crop.

A fox is taking all the crops! Draw an X over the crop the fox is taking away. Circle what is left. Then complete each number sentence.

1. I'm going to take away 3!

$6 - 3 = \underline{3}$

2. I'm going to take away 8!

$\underline{} - \underline{} = \underline{}$

3. I'm going to take away 4!

$\underline{} - \underline{} = \underline{}$

Assessment

Chapter 12 Review

In this chapter, your child studied similar sounding words, subtracting numbers through 6, and subtracting numbers through 12.

Your child learned:
- Recognition of rhyming words.
- Subtraction.

Do the following activities to review what your child has learned. If your child is having difficulty in any of the areas below, go back through the pages of this chapter with your child. With the additional activities listed below, you can also review and reinforce the skills covered in this chapter.

1. Have your child fill in the blanks.

$$12 - 6 = \underline{\quad} \qquad \underline{\quad} - 2 = 2 \qquad 9 - \underline{\quad} = 8$$

$$10 - \underline{\quad} = 2 \qquad 6 - 3 = \underline{\quad} \qquad \underline{\quad} - 7 = 4$$

2. Circle the word pairs that rhyme.

BAT, CAT	POT, PIG	BUG, TUB
BALL, SUN	FAN, MAN	TEN, HEN

3. Have your child write 3 words that rhyme with BAT.

Additional Activities

Here are some simple and fun things you can do with your child to practice what you have worked on in this chapter. To help reinforce what was learned in this chapter, try these activities.

1. Have your child count the number of doors in your house. Is the number more or less than 12?
2. Ask your child to write out 6 subtraction number problems only using the numbers between 1 and 12. Tell your child that they are writing these out for you to solve.
3. Have your child tell you what their 3 favorite toys are and then try to think of words that rhyme with the toy.

Chapter 13

Today's lesson will be lots of fun as we join Bogart and Sam while they visit their playhouse!

While they explore, you will have a good time learning:
- Rhyming
- Subtracting numbers 1-12 in a problem

Now let's see what's happening at the playhouse!

Rhyming Words

Quincy sees a bat in the cave. Write a word that rhymes with **bat** on the lines below. Draw a picture of the word you write.

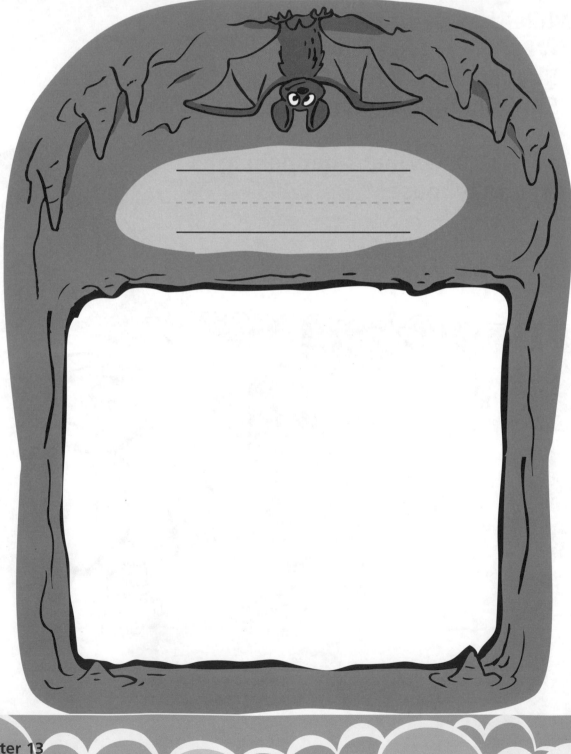

Rhyming Words

Write a word that rhymes with each word below.
Draw a picture for each word you write.

pet

cot

fun

Subtracting Numbers through 12

The animals on the farm are playing hide and seek! Take some of them away and help them hide by circling them. Then write a number sentence that shows what you subtracted.

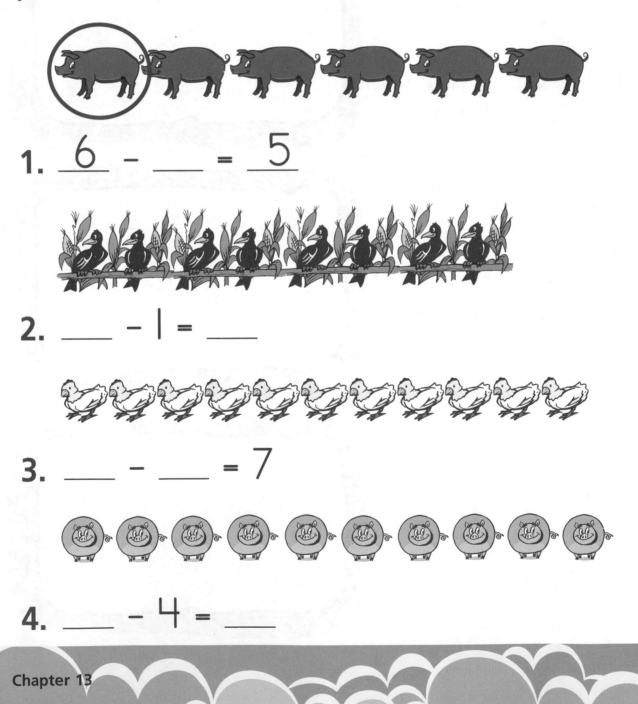

1. __6__ – ____ = __5__

2. ____ – 1 = ____

3. ____ – ____ = 7

4. ____ – 4 = ____

Which Show Subtraction?

Circle the operations that show subtraction.

A – sign means to subtract.

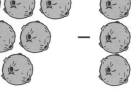

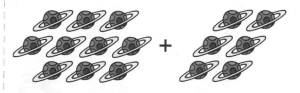

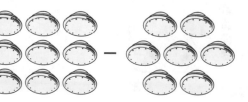

Modeling Problems

Draw a line from each set of cube units to its description.

Remember, each cube unit stands for 1.

A.

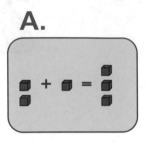

1. Subtract 2 cube units from 4 cube units to get 2 cube units.

B.

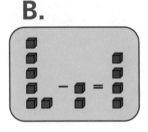

2. Subtract 4 cube units from 5 cube units to get 1 cube unit.

C.

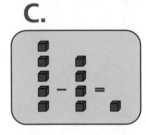

3. Add 1 cube unit to 2 cube units to get 3 cube units.

D.

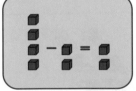

4. Add 2 cube units to 3 cube units to get 5 cube units.

E.

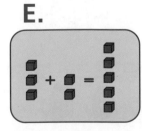

5. Subtract 2 cube units from 6 cube units to get 4 cube units.

That's a lot of cubes!

Assessment

Chapter 13 Review

In this chapter, your child studied rhyming words, subtracting numbers through 12, identifying modeling problems, and recognizing subtraction.

Your child learned:
- Recognition of rhyming words.
- Subtraction.
- Visual recognition of subtraction problems.

The following activities will provide a review of what your child has learned. If he or she has any difficulty in any of the areas below, go back through the pages of this chapter with your child. You can also review and reinforce the skills in this section with the additional activities listed below.

1. Have your child draw a picture of cat, bug, hat and tub. Then ask your child to circle the pictures that rhyme.

2. Have your child complete these number sentences:

   $12 - 2 =$ ___ $10 - 4 =$ ___ $1 - 1 =$ ___ $8 - 3 =$ ___ $5 - 0 =$ ___

3. Have your child fill in the blanks.

   $8 -$ ___ $= 4$ $1 -$ ___ $= 1$ $12 -$ ___ $= 12$ $3 -$ ___ $= 2$ $9 -$ ___ $= 4$

Additional Activities

Here are some simple and fun things you can do with your child to practice what you have worked on in this chapter. To help reinforce what was learned in this chapter, try these activities.

1. Have your child cut out pictures from a magazine that are rhymes (such as a boat and a coat).
2. With your child, use index cards to make flash cards of - , +, and = symbols. Use them in the next activity.
3. Give your child 12 items (such as marbles or M&M's). Now separate the items in different combinations and have your child write a number sentence that shows what you subtracted.

Chapter 14

Today's lesson will be lots of fun as we join Rosa and Quincy while they explore the solar system!

While they explore, you will have a good time learning:
• Rhyming
• Word problems

Now let's see what's going on deep in space!

Rhyming Words

Help Bogart name each picture with two words that rhyme. Write the words on the lines.

b u g   h u g

b a t   h a t

m a p   h a t

t a t   c a t

I can think of another one! A fish that grants wishes is a wish fish!

Rhyming Words

Look at the pictures in each row and color the ones whose names rhyme.

Say the names of the pictures. Listen to see if they rhyme.

shell

dog

bell

pie

pot

eye

house

king

ring

Modeling Problems

Draw a line from each description to
the equation that means the same thing.

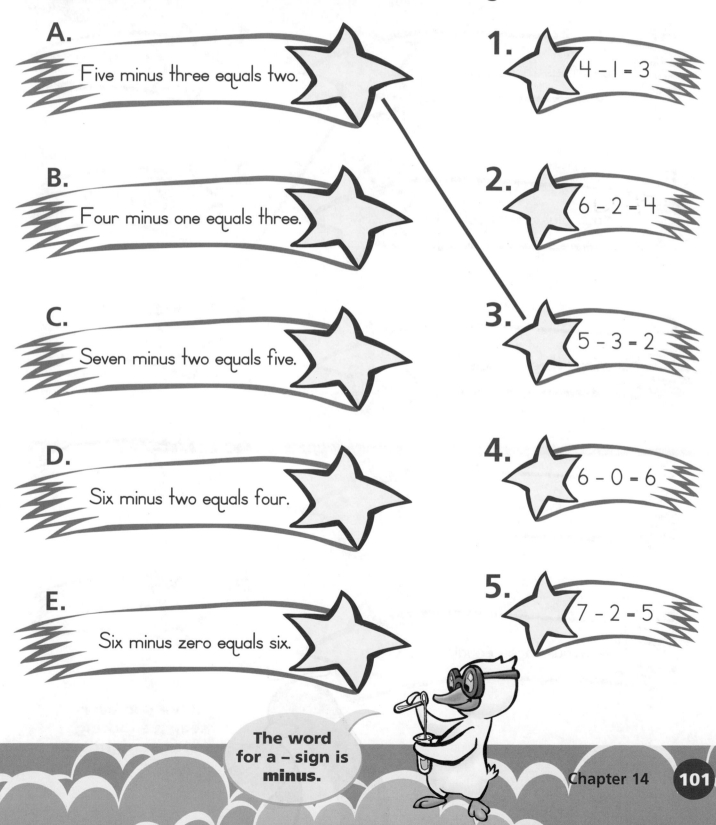

A. Five minus three equals two.

B. Four minus one equals three.

C. Seven minus two equals five.

D. Six minus two equals four.

E. Six minus zero equals six.

1. 4 – 1 = 3

2. 6 – 2 = 4

3. 5 – 3 = 2

4. 6 – 0 = 6

5. 7 – 2 = 5

The word
for a – sign is
minus.

Modeling Problems

Some of these are addition equations, and some are subtraction equations.

Draw a line from each description to the equation that means the same thing.

A. Three minus three equals zero.

B. Four plus one equals five.

C. Six minus three equals three.

D. One plus one equals two.

E. Five minus three equals two.

1. $6 - 3 = 3$

2. $1 + 1 = 2$

3. $3 - 3 = 0$

4. $5 - 3 = 2$

5. $4 + 1 = 5$

Have you ever seen a shooting star at night?

Modeling Problems

Draw a picture that describes each equation.
Use the stars shown.

5 – 2 = 3

6 – 3 = 3

3 – 1 = 2

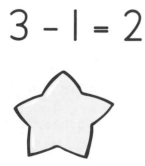

There are a lot of stars in a galaxy!

Assessment

Chapter 14 Review

In this chapter, your child studied rhyming words and identifying modeling problems. Because repetition is an effective method to reinforce learning, some exercises in this chapter were similar.

Your child learned:
- Recognition of rhyming words.
- Subtraction.
- Visual recognition of subtraction problems.

To review what your child has learned, do the activities below. Review the pages of this chapter with your child if he or she is having difficulty in any of the areas below. You can also review and reinforce the skills in this section with the additional activities listed below.

1. On a separate piece of paper, have your child write the number equation for:

- Twelve minus two equals ten
- Three minus zero equals
- Nine minus five equals
- Seven minus six equals

2. On a separate sheet of paper, have your child write out the word equations for:

$$3 - 0 = 3 \quad 10 - 9 = 1 \quad 5 - 2 = 3$$

3. On a separate sheet of paper, have your child draw a picture of these rhyming words:

Wish   Fish
Wet   Net
Pet   Vet

Additional Activities
Here are some interactive ways you and your child can practice what you have worked on in this chapter. These activities will reinforce the skills your child studied on the previous pages.

1. Read a book with rhyming words to your child and have him/her tell you the words that rhyme on each page.
2. Using index cards, make flash cards for numbers 1 through 12. Make the cards using the symbol, word, and number of dots for each number.

Example:

3. Using the symbol cards you made in Chapter 13 and your number cards, put together different equations to solve.

Chapter 15

Today's lesson will be lots of fun as we join Rosa and Quincy while they explore the jungle!

While they explore, you will have a good time learning:
- Rhyming
- Addition and subtraction symbols
- Adding and subtracting numbers 1-12 in a problem

Now let's see what's going on in the jungle!

Rhyming Words

Help Bogart create a picture story. In each box below, draw pictures of words that rhyme.

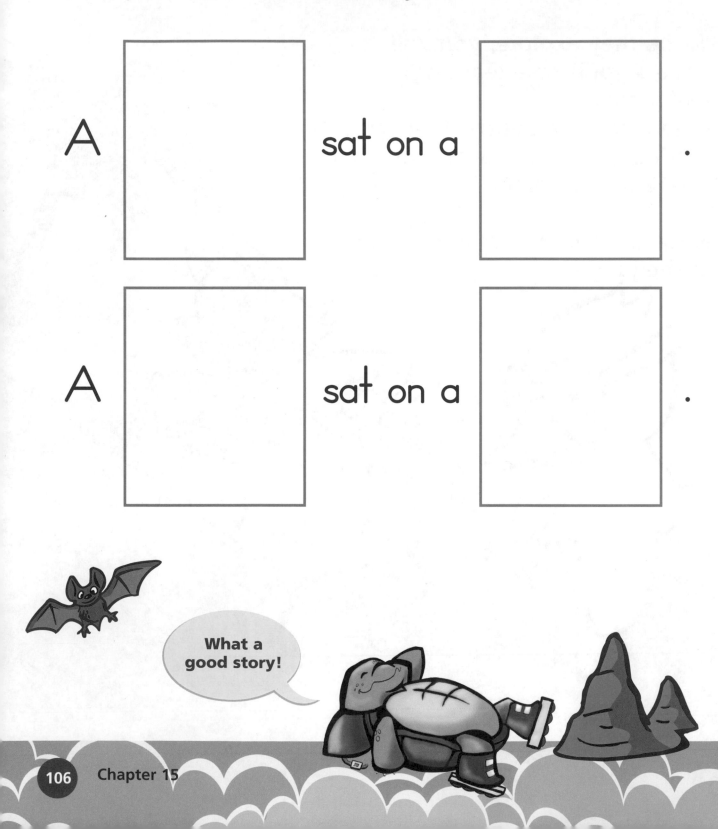

A [ ] sat on a [ ] .

A [ ] sat on a [ ] .

What a good story!

Rhyming Words

Write each word in the box on the line next to the word it rhymes with below.

box	bug	mat	cot

rug _____

fox _____

dot _____

rat _____

I think these are fun!

Rhyming Words

It's time to rhyme!

Make up your own rhymes using the letters below!
Then draw pictures to illustrate your words.

ad   ad

op   op

Talking About Things

Play this game with a friend.
Help Marco get to the carrot.

Pick a number between 1 and 10. Add 1 as you pass each + sign and subtract 1 as you pass each − sign.

Terrific!

Adding and Subtracting Numbers through 12

Add or subtract to answer each problem.

1. $9 - 5 = $ ___

2. $6 + 6 = $ ___

3. $3 + 6 = $ ___

4. $9 - 2 = $ ___

5. $11 + 0 = $ ___

6. $4 + 1 = $ ___

Match the numbers on the turkey to the answers above. Color the numbered sections the same color of the number sentence they match.

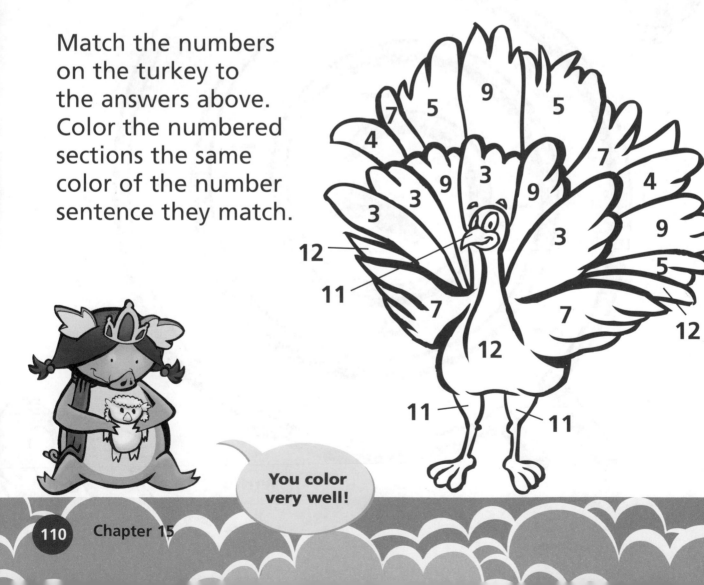

You color very well!

Assessment

Chapter 15 Review

In this chapter, your child studied rhyming words and adding and subtracting numbers through 12. Because repetition is an effective method to reinforce learning, some exercises in this chapter were similar.

Your child learned:
- Recognition of rhyming words.
- Subtraction.
- Addition.

Do the following activities to review what your child has learned. If your child is having difficulty in any of the areas below, go back through the pages of this chapter with your child. With the additional activities listed below, you can also review and reinforce the skills covered in this chapter.

1. Have your child fill in the blanks to make these words rhyme:

___AT   ___AT   ___ET   ___ET   ___IG   ___IG

2. Give your child a number between 1 and 12. Using the same rules that are on page 109, do the following problems. (• represents the number your child selects.)

    • -, +, - = ___   • +, +, + = ___   • -, -, - = ___

3. Ask your child to solve the following problems:

    10 + 2 = ___   11 – 3 = ___   7 + 3 = ___
    5 + 6 = ___   4 – 2 = ___   2 + 8 = ___

Additional Activities

Here are some simple and fun things you can do with your child to practice what you have worked on in this chapter. To help reinforce what was learned in this chapter, try these activities.

1. Give your child two words that rhyme with each other, then ask your child to write out both words.
2. Using the two rhyming words from the activity you just did, have your child put the words in a sentence. You can have your child verbally say or write the sentence.
3. Make four more – and + flash cards, and use them with the 1 through 12 flash cards to play this game. Place the cards in two stacks in front of your child with all of the – and + cards in one stack and the number cards in the other. Tell him/her to pick one card from the 1 through 12 stack. Next, have him/her pick a card from the -, + stack. Add 1 to the number card drawn for each + card and subtract 1 from the number card drawn for each – card. Go through all of the + and - cards. Have your child write down the final number.

Chapter 16

Everybody loves to visit the farm! There is always something for everyone to do.

While they explore, you will have a good time learning about:
• The letter I
• The number 7

Syllables

Bogart looks at the map to see how to get to the cave. Draw lines between the words with one syllable to help him get back to the cave.

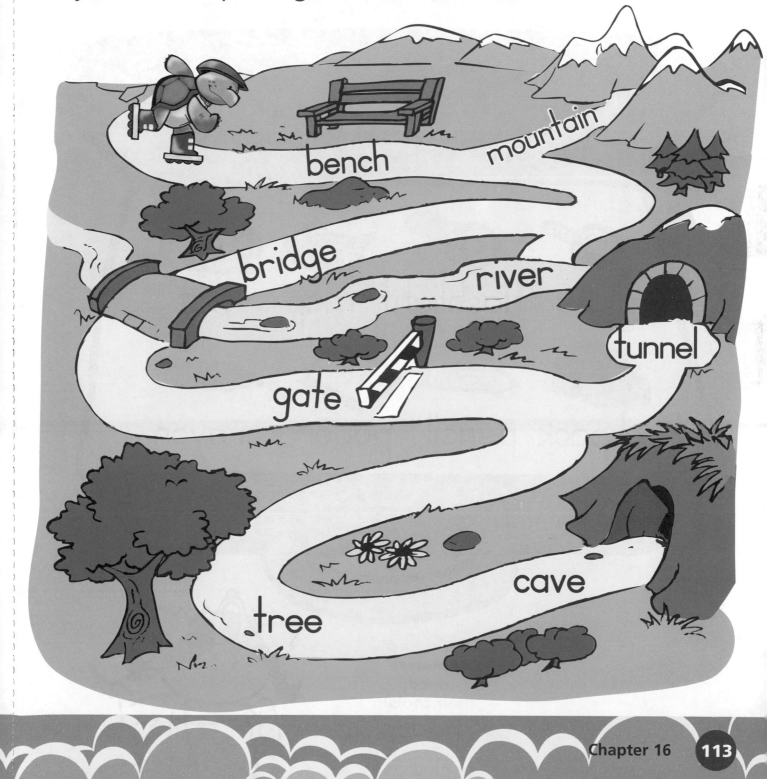

Syllables

Here are some of the things Paige and Sam have in their explorer's kit. Circle each word with one syllable. Underline each word with two syllables.

glass   flashlight   map   hat

backpack   pencil   paper   crayon

Explorers need their tools!

Syllables

As they explore the cave, Paige and Sam see great animal pictures! Write **1**, **2**, or **3** in each box to tell how many syllables are in the word.

The word **puppy** has two syllables!

monkey

kangaroo

pig

whale

fish

tiger

Matching Addition and Subtraction Problems

Help Quincy feed the animals. Solve each number sentence. Then draw a line to match each addition problem to the subtraction problem with the same answer.

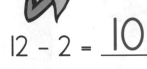

$5 + 5 = \underline{10}$

$12 - 2 = \underline{10}$

$4 + 4 = \underline{}$

$6 + 3 = \underline{}$

$12 - 3 = \underline{}$

$12 - 4 = \underline{}$

$7 + 5 = \underline{}$

$12 - 0 = \underline{}$

Identifying Fact Families

Add and subtract to create a fact family.

A **fact family** is a group of number sentences that shows how three or more numbers are related.

1. $2 + 1 = 3$

2. $3 - 2 = 1$

3. $1 + 2 = 3$

4. $3 - 1 = \underline{2}$

5. $3 + 2 = \underline{}$

6. $5 - 2 = \underline{}$

7. $2 + 3 = \underline{}$

8. $5 - 3 = \underline{}$

9. $2 + \underline{} = \underline{}$

10. $\underline{} - 2 = \underline{}$

11. $\underline{} + 2 = \underline{}$

12. $4 - \underline{} = \underline{}$

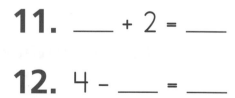

The more the merrier!

Assessment

Chapter 16 Review

In this chapter, your child studied syllables, addition and subtraction problems, and fact families. Because repetition is an effective method to reinforce learning, some exercises in this chapter were similar.

Your child learned:
- The difference between one and two syllables.
- Addition and subtraction.
- Identification of fact families.

To review what your child has learned, have your child do the activities below. Review the pages of this chapter with your child if he or she is having difficulty in any of the areas below. You can also review and reinforce the skills in this section with the additional activities listed below.

1. Have your child circle the words with one syllable.

LAMP   MONDAY   BOOK   LIGHT   HAPPY

2. Ask your child to solve the following problems to complete the fact family:

$$4 + 2 = \underline{\quad} \qquad 6 - 2 = \underline{\quad} \qquad 2 + 4 = \underline{\quad} \qquad 6 - 4 = \underline{\quad}$$

3. Have your child write the fact family for:

9, 4, 5

Additional Activities

Here are some simple and fun activities you can do with your child to practice what you have worked on in this chapter. These activities will reinforce the skills your child studied on the previous pages.

1. Have your child look around the house and identify objects that are one-syllable words.
2. Ask your child to say or write as many 1, 2, or 3-syllable words as he/she can in one minute.
3. Give your child two numbers, or have him/her pick two numbers using the 1 through 12 cards. Have him/her write a fact family using the two numbers to figure out the third number.

Chapter 17

Today's lesson will be lots of fun as we join Quincy and friends while they visit the zoo!

While they explore, you will have a good time learning:
- Sight words
- Fact families
- Addition and subtraction

Sight Words

Circle the word **you** in each sentence.

Are you a frog?

Are you a deer?

Are you a raccoon?

Are you a lizard?

Are you a kid?

I think **you** are just great!

This page completed by: _____

Sight Words

Read the postcard Sam wrote to a friend.
Underline the word **have** each time you see it.

I have a ___ .

I have a ___ .

I have a ___ .

I have fun!

Sam

I like to stay in touch with my friends!

Fact Families

Use addition or subtraction to create fact families.

Remember, a fact family is a group of number sentences that shows how three or more numbers are related.

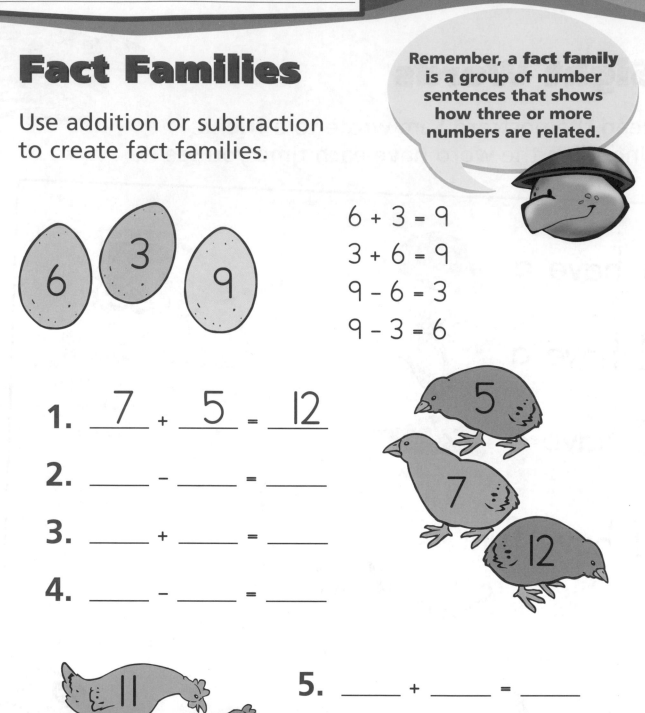

$6 + 3 = 9$
$3 + 6 = 9$
$9 - 6 = 3$
$9 - 3 = 6$

1. __7__ + __5__ = __12__

2. ____ - ____ = ____

3. ____ + ____ = ____

4. ____ - ____ = ____

5. ____ + ____ = ____

6. ____ - ____ = ____

7. ____ + ____ = ____

8. __11__ - __6__ = __5__

Finding the Missing Number

Draw a line from each fact family to the number that is missing from it.

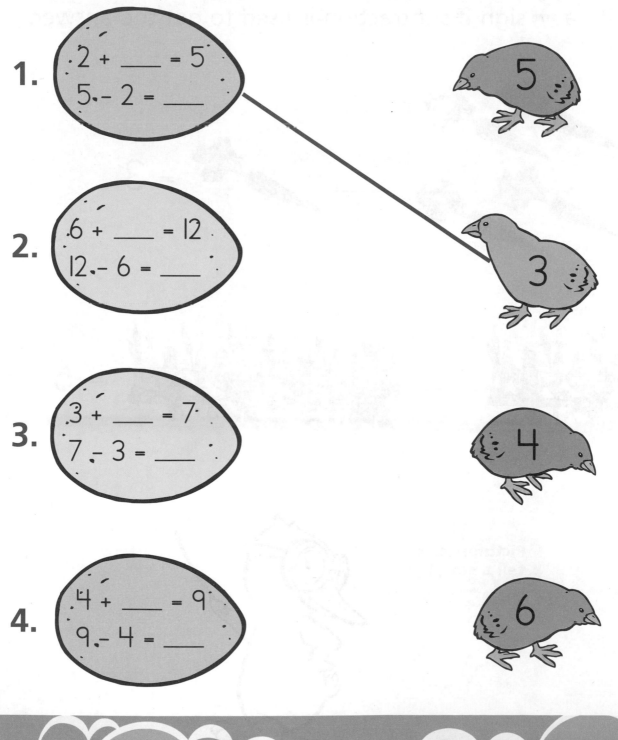

1. 2 + ___ = 5
   5 – 2 = ___

2. 6 + ___ = 12
   12 – 6 = ___

3. 3 + ___ = 7
   7 – 3 = ___

4. 4 + ___ = 9
   9 – 4 = ___

5

3

4

6

Identifying Addition and Subtraction

Write a **+** sign if addition is used to get the answer.
Write a **—** sign if subtraction is used to get the answer.

Pictures can tell a story!

Assessment

Chapter 17 Review

In this chapter, your child studied sight words, fact families, and addition and subtraction.

Your child learned:
- Recognition of sight words.
- Addition and subtraction.
- Comprehension of fact families.

The following activities will provide a review of what your child has learned. If he or she has any difficulty in any of the areas below, go back through the pages of this chapter with your child. You can also review and reinforce the skills in this section with the additional activities listed below.

1. Have your child find the missing number.

$$a.\ 4 + \underline{\ \ \ } = 8 \qquad\qquad b.\ 4 + \underline{\ \ \ } = 12$$
$$8 - 4 = \underline{\ \ \ } \qquad\qquad\qquad 12 - \underline{\ \ \ } = 4$$

2. Ask your child to use a + or − to complete the number equation.

$$5 \underline{\ \ \ } 2 = 3 \qquad 1 \underline{\ \ \ } 3 = 4$$
$$8 \underline{\ \ \ } 1 = 9 \qquad 7 \underline{\ \ \ } 5 = 12$$

3. Have your child write the fact family for: 7, 2, 5

Additional Activities

Below are some interactive ways you and your child can practice what you have worked on in this chapter. These activities will reinforce the skills your child studied on the previous pages.

1. Read a favorite story to your child. Pick a word that appears several times on a page and ask your child to point to that word.

2. Using index cards, help your child make flash cards of these sight words:

I, YOU, A, HAVE, and IS

3. Give your child five index cards and ask him/her to draw a different picture on each one. Help your child write the word for each picture.

Chapter 18

Today's lesson will be lots of fun as we join Quincy and Sam while they work in the garden!

While they explore, you will have a good time learning:
• Sight words
• Illustrating addition and subtraction problems
• Addition and subtraction symbols

Now let's see what's going on in the garden!

Sight Words

Color the spaces with the word **go.** Use a green crayon.

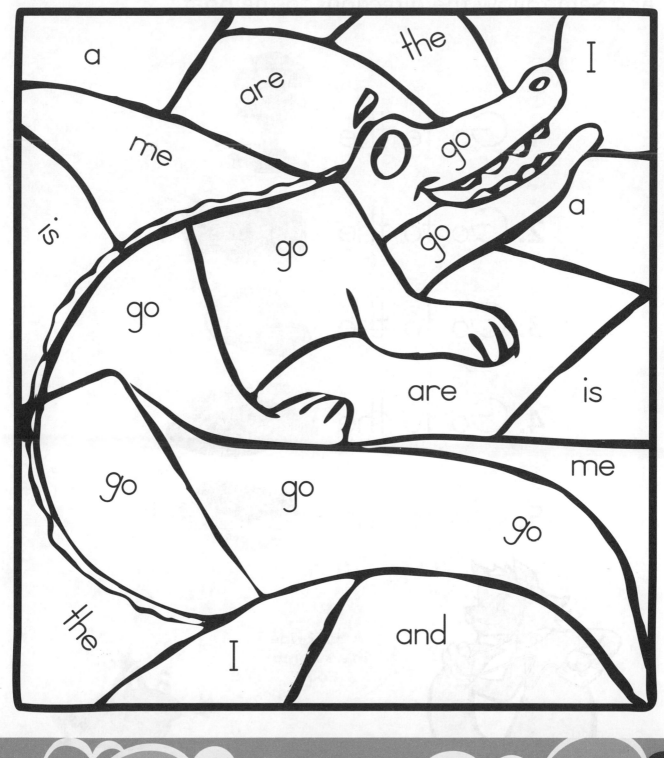

Sight Words

Circle the word **to** in each sentence. Then draw lines to connect the pictures on the next page to help Marco and Sam follow the directions to the boat.

1. Go to the   .

2. Go to the   .

3. Go to the   .

4. Go to the   .

5. Go to the   !

A boat ride in a swamp! Cool!

Drawing Pictures that Show Addition and Subtraction

Draw a picture that shows addition using at least one of the above pictures.

Write a number sentence that explains what you drew.

___ + ___ = ___

Draw a picture that shows subtraction using at least one of the above pictures.

You draw very well!

Write a number sentence that explains what you drew.

___ - ___ = ___

130   Chapter 18

Which is Described, Addition or Subtraction?

Circle the symbol that correctly completes each problem.

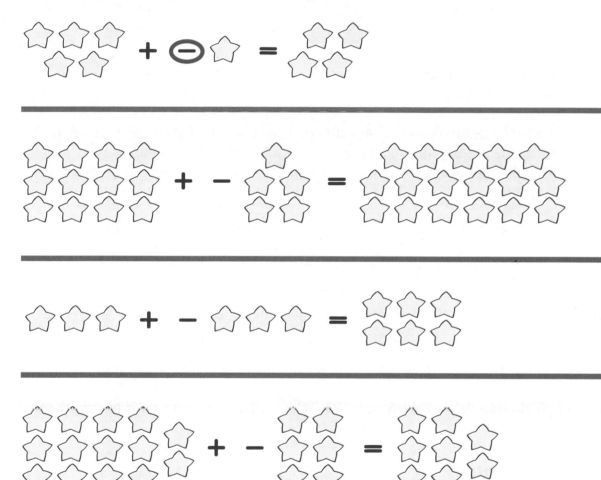

Terrific!

Assessment

Chapter 18 Review

In this chapter, your child studied sight words, visualizing addition and subtraction, and modeling problems.

Your child learned:
- Recognition of sight words.
- Visualization of addition and subtraction.
- Modeling problems.

Do the following activities to review what your child has learned. If your child is having difficulty in any of the areas below, go back through the pages of this chapter with your child. With the additional activities listed below, you can also review and reinforce the skills covered in this chapter.

1. Ask your child to circle the correct symbol (+ or -) to complete each problem.

$$10 + - 3 = 13 \quad 14 + - 5 = 9 \quad 8 + - 5 = 13 \quad 11 + - 1 = 10$$

2. Have your child solve:

$$10 + 5 = \underline{\quad} \qquad 9 + 4 = \underline{\quad} \qquad 8 - 7 = \underline{\quad} \qquad 4 + 4 = \underline{\quad}$$
$$3 - 3 = \underline{\quad} \qquad 16 - 1 = \underline{\quad} \qquad 12 + 2 = \underline{\quad} \qquad 5 - 2 = \underline{\quad}$$

3. Have your child write these sight words: GO, TO, and THE. Ask your child to use these words in sentences.

Additional Activities
Here are some simple and fun activities you can do with your child to practice what you have worked on in this chapter. These activities will reinforce the skills your child studied on the previous pages.

1. Using index cards, make flash cards for these sight words: THE, GO, AND, TO, and ARE. Add these to the sight word cards you made in Chapter 17.
2. Use star stickers to have your child illustrate addition and subtraction number sentences.
3. Give your child five index cards; ask him or her to draw a different picture on each one. Help your child write the word for each picture. Combine these with the five cards you did in Chapter 17.

Chapter 19

Today's lesson will be lots of fun as we join Quincy and Paige as they walk in the forest!

While they explore, you will have a good time learning:
- Sight words
- Identifying shapes

Now let's see what's going on in the forest!

This page completed by:

Sight Words

See how many times you can find the word **do** in this puzzle. Circle the word each time you find it. Look for words that go ➡ and ⬇ .

d	o	a	t
c	l	d	z
d	r	o	b
o	m	s	d
p	d	o	o

Sight Words

Circle the word **said** each time you see it.

"There is the alligator!" Sam said. "There it is," the man said.

"It is big!" said Sam. "It is," the man said.

"Can I pet it?" Sam asked. "Do not!" said the man.

Finding Hexagons and Octagons

Hexagons have six sides.
Color the hexagons blue.
Octagons have eight sides.
Color the octagons red.

Hexagons look like: , and octagons look like: .

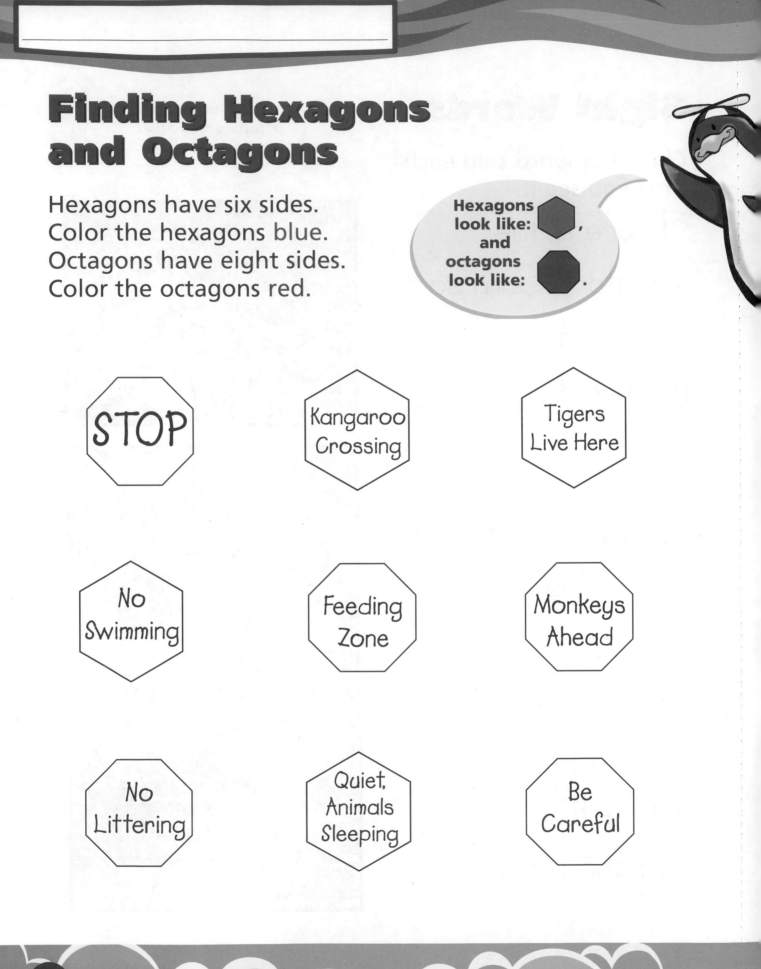

Picturing Things

Draw an *X* over the 10 shapes that you find in the tree.

Remember,
a circle looks like: ●,
a trapezoid looks like: ▱,
a triangle looks like: △,
a rectangle looks like: ▭,
an octagon looks like: ⬣,
a hexagon looks like: ⬡.

How many circles did you find? _____

How many trapezoids did you find? _____

How many triangles did you find? _____

How many rectangles did you find? _____

How many octagons did you find? _____

How many hexagons did you find? _____

Drawing Shapes from Their Names

Let's draw some shapes!

Draw a **square** around the elephant.

Draw a **triangle** around the elephant.

Draw a **hexagon** around the elephant.

Draw a **trapezoid** around the elephant.

Shapes are fun!

Assessment

Chapter 19 Review

In this chapter, your child studied sight words and different shapes.

Your child learned:
- Recognition of sight words.
- Identification of shapes.
- Visualization of shapes within objects.

To review what your child has learned, do the 3 activities below with him/her. If your child is having difficulty in any of the areas below, go back and review the pages with him or her. You can also review and reinforce the skills in this section with the additional activities listed below.

1. Ask your child when you would use the word "said" in a sentence.

2. Ask your child how many sides there are to a hexagon and to an octagon.

3. Ask your child to identify these shapes:

Additional Activities
Here are some simple and fun activities you can do with your child to practice what you have worked on in Chapter 19. These activities will reinforce the skills your child learned on the previous pages.

1. Direct your child to put together sentences using the 10 sight-word flash cards and the 10 picture-word flash cards you made in earlier chapter activities.
2. Have your child draw as many different shapes as he or she can on construction paper. Now ask your child to cut out the shapes they have drawn.
3. The next time you take your child to a store, see how many different shapes he/she can find.

Chapter 20

Today's lesson will be lots of fun as we join Sam while he works driving a tractor!

While he explores, you will have a good time learning:
• Sight words
• Identifying solid shapes

Now let's see what's going on at the zoo!

Sight Words

Find and circle the word in each box that belongs in the sentence.

This is one hot day!

Rosa

Quincy

Sam

Paige

The sun | is   do | hot.

Paige and Sam | my   are | sleepy.

Rosa has | said   a | hat.

Quincy and Sam | do   to | not have hats.

Sight Words

Draw a line to match the words on the birds to the words on the branches.

Look at each word carefully.

have

said

go

do

do

go

said

have

Identifying Congruent Shapes

Draw a line between the shapes that are **exactly** the same.

Congruent shapes are shapes that are the same size and shape.

Congruent is a fun word to say!

Finding Cubes

Find the sections that have cubes in them.
Color the sections that have cubes green.

A cube looks like:

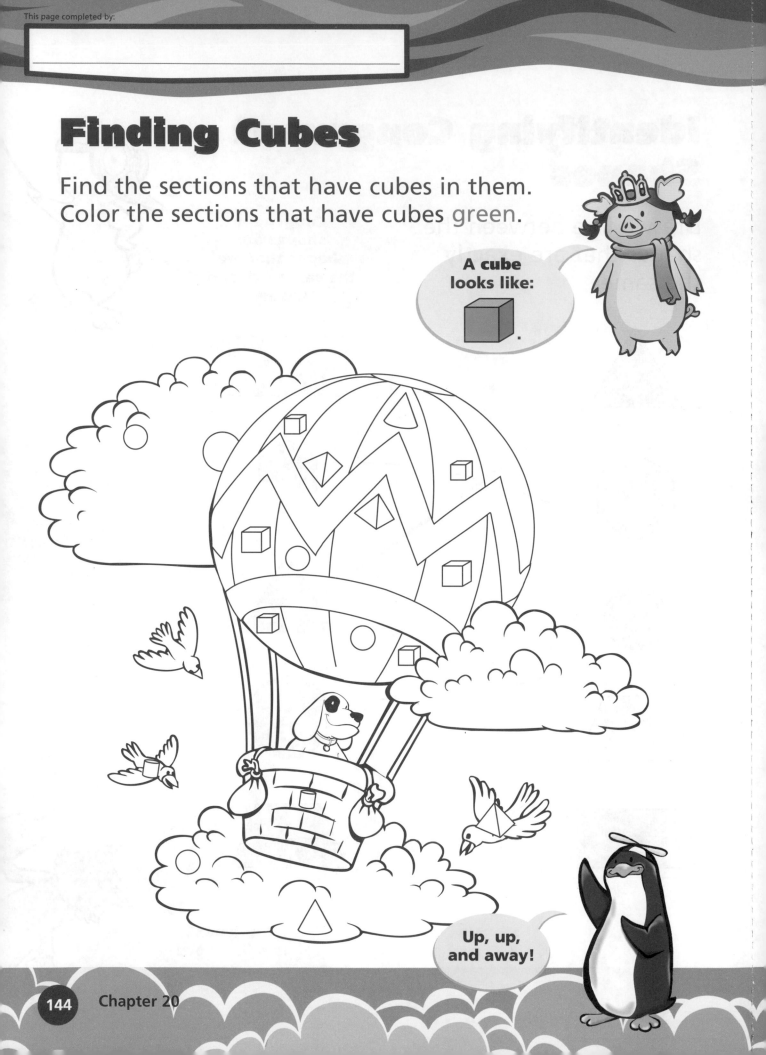

Up, up, and away!

Drawing Cubes

Trace the cubes Bogart passes in the maze.

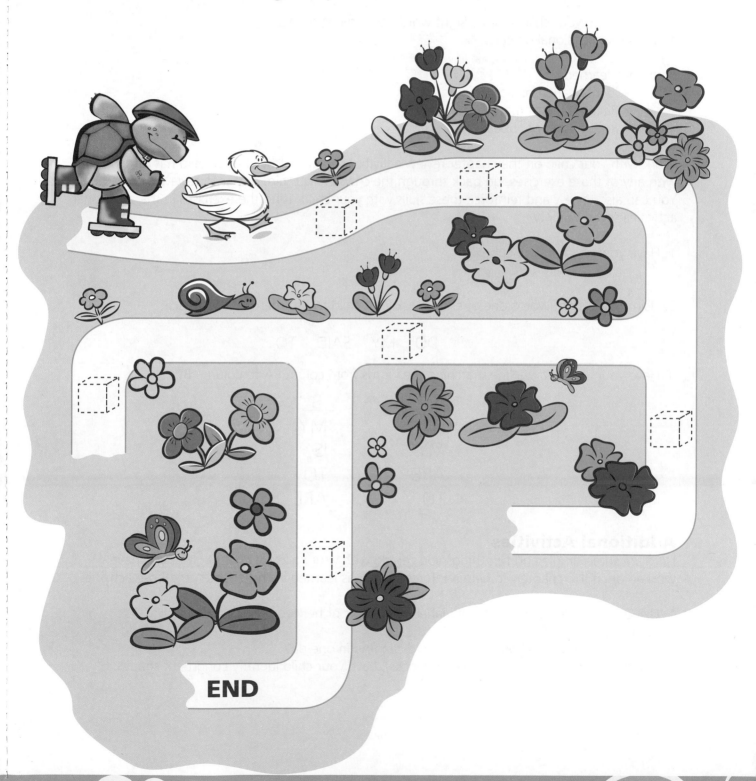

END

Assessment

Chapter 20 Review

In this chapter, your child studied sight words, congruent shapes, and three-dimensional objects.

Your child learned:
- Identification of sight words.
- Recognition of matching shapes.
- Recognition of cubes.

Work with your child on the chapter review activities shown below. If your child has difficulty with any of these exercises, go back through the chapter with him or her to review the material. You can also review and reinforce these skills with your child using the exercises in the additional activities section below.

1. Have your child draw a cube.

2. Using these sight words one at a time, ask your child to use them in a sentence.

DO   MY   SAID   TO

3. Have your child draw a line matching the words from column A to column B.

A	B
IS	MY
MY	IS
ARE	TO
TO	ARE

Additional Activities

Here are some simple and fun things you can do with your child to practice what you have worked on in this chapter. To help reinforce what was learned in this chapter, try these activities.

1. Using index cards, help your child label items in his or her room (such as bed, door, window, and floor).
2. See how many cubes you and your child can find in one day.
3. Using shape blocks (such as building blocks), have your child identify congruent shapes.

Chapter 21

Today's lesson will be lots of fun as we join Rosa dancing in the desert!

While she explores, you will have a good time learning:
- Word comprehension
- Sight words
- Identifying solid shapes

Now let's see what's going on in the desert!

Good work!

Word Meanings

Circle the word that tells you what each animal is doing.

kick   throw

sit   stand

sleep   run

Word Meanings

Read each sentence. What do the underlined words mean? Write each underlined word under the picture it matches.

Pam lost her balloon. Now she is <u>sad</u>.

_____
- - - - - - - - - - - -
_____

Pam won the race! She is <u>happy</u>!

_____
- - - - - - - - - - - -
_____

Pam had a busy day. She is <u>tired</u>.

_____
- - - - - - - - - - - -
_____

Recognizing Words

Read the words in the list below. Then find the words in the puzzle. Cross out the words on the list as you find them.

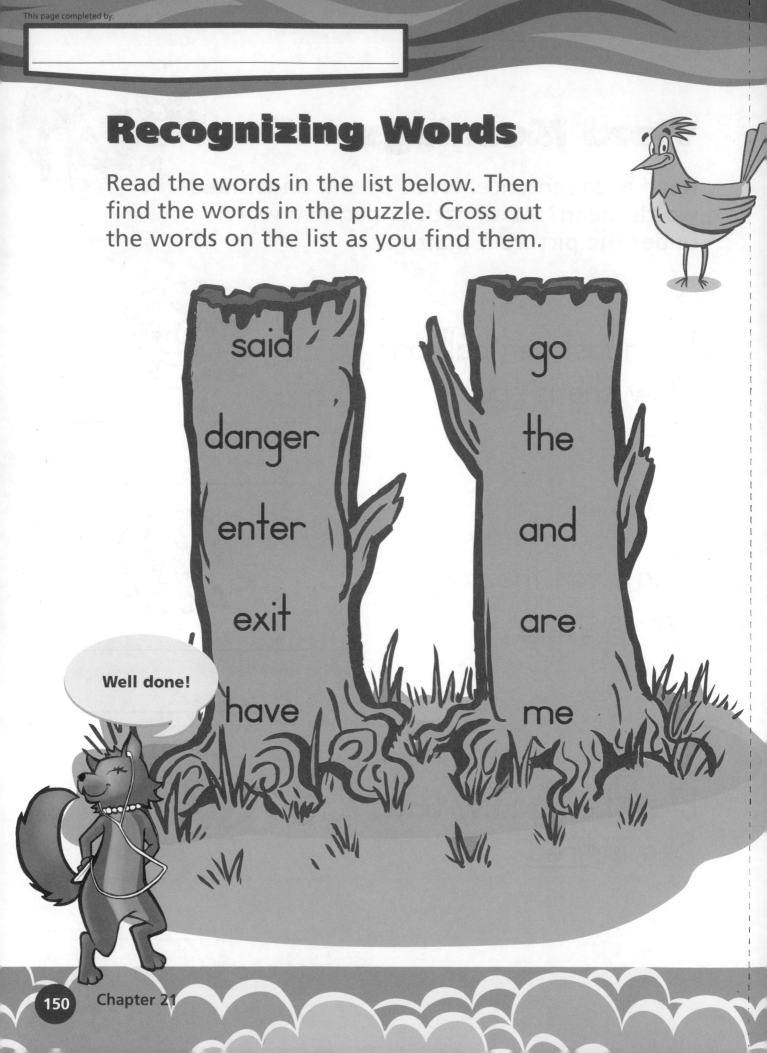

said

danger

enter

exit

have

go

the

and

are

me

Well done!

Try looking for the first letter of each word.

Look for words that go ➡ and ⬇ .

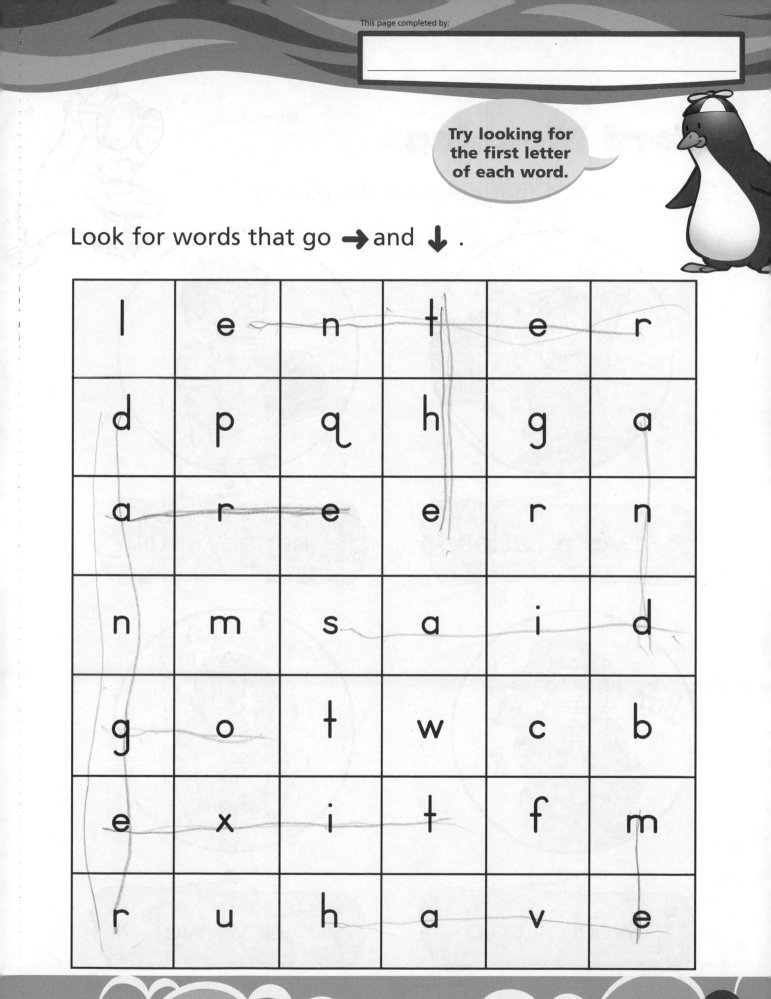

l	e	n	t	e	r
d	p	q	h	g	a
a	r	e	e	r	n
n	m	s	a	i	d
g	o	t	w	c	b
e	x	i	t	f	m
r	u	h	a	v	e

Word Meanings

Nice work!

Circle the word that describes the picture.

awake   asleep

hungry   full

warm   cold

dry   wet

Assessment

Chapter 21 Review

In this chapter, your child studied word recognition, word meanings, and shape identification.

Your child learned:
- Comprehension of words.
- Recognition of words.
- Differentiation of objects.

Do the following activities to review what your child has learned. If your child is having difficulty in any of the areas below, go back through the pages of this chapter with your child. With the additional activities listed below, you can also review and reinforce the skills covered in this chapter.

1. On a separate sheet of paper, have your child draw faces that are SAD, HAPPY, and MAD.

2. Ask your child to tell you the opposite of each word.

ASLEEP   WARM   FULL   DRY

3. Ask your child to identify this shape.

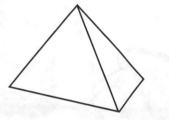

Additional Activities

Here are some simple and fun things you can do with your child to practice what you have worked on in this chapter. To help reinforce what was learned in this chapter, try these activities.

1. Play the game Simon Says.
2. Do a project together with your child: make a word wall using magazine pictures.
3. Find a book of age-appropriate word search puzzles and keep it in your car for your child to use during long trips or waits in the doctor's office.

Chapter 22

Today's lesson will be lots of fun as we join Bogart and Sam while they soar high in the sky!

While they explore, you will have a good time learning:
• Nouns
• Identifying solid shapes

Now let's see what's going on in the clouds!

Naming Words: People

Underline the words that name people.
Then color the picture!

table

store

baby

Mom

Dad

Meg

Joe

bench

Naming Words: People

Help Sam find some more naming words.
Circle each word that names a person.

teacher

football

doctor

sailor

apple

top

pilot

queen

kite

I know some naming words for people: **baker, painter,** and **police officer.**

Naming Words: People

Read the sentences. Draw lines to match the naming words to the people in the picture.

The boy has a net.   The girl has a box.

The baby has a hat.   The woman has a pen.

Naming Words: Things

Look at the picture. Then finish the sentences by writing the names of things you see in the desert on the lines.

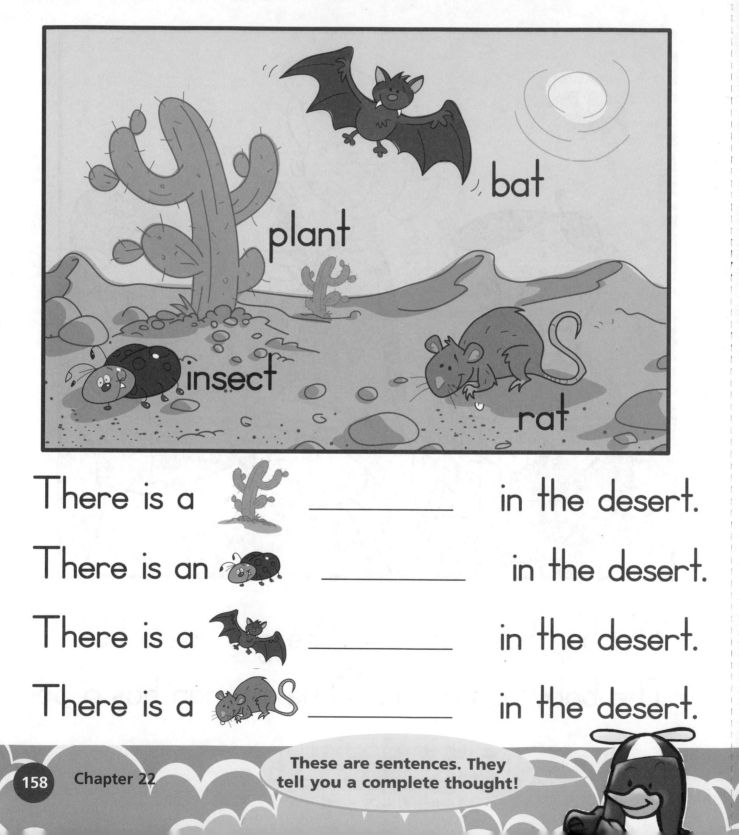

bat

plant

insect

rat

There is a _____ in the desert.

There is an _____ in the desert.

There is a _____ in the desert.

There is a _____ in the desert.

These are sentences. They tell you a complete thought!

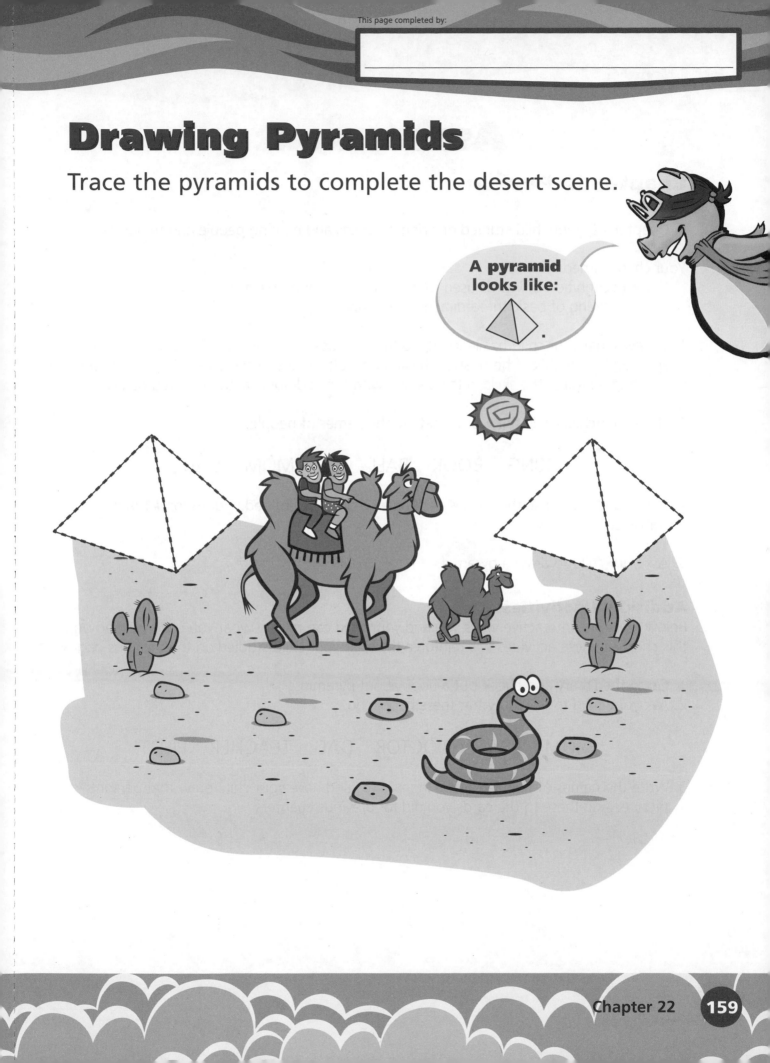

Drawing Pyramids

Trace the pyramids to complete the desert scene.

A pyramid looks like:

Assessment

Chapter 22 Review

In Chapter 22, your child studied drawing pyramids and naming people and things.

Your child learned:
- Recognition of words used to identify people and objects.
- Drawing of basic three-dimensional shapes.

To review what your child has learned, do the activities below. Review the pages of this chapter with your child if he or she is having difficulty in any of the areas below. You can also review and reinforce the skills in this section with the additional activities listed below.

1. Have your child circle the words that are the names of people.

KING   BOOK   BALL   PIG   MOM   DAD

2. Ask your child to use the names of people he or she identified in question #1 in a sentence.

3. Ask your child to draw a pyramid.

Additional Activities

Below are some interactive ways you and your child can review what you have worked on in this chapter. These activities will reinforce the skills your child studied on the previous pages.

1. Go to the library and check out a book about pyramids.
2. Ask your child to tell you what these people do.

MOM   BABY   DOCTOR   DAD   TEACHER   PILOT

3. Write the names of people on five index cards and have your child draw that person's picture. Add these to the cards you did for previous chapters.

Chapter 23

Today's lesson will be lots of fun as we join Paige and Sam while they explore the cave!

While they explore, you will have a good time learning:
- Completing sentences
- Sight words
- Identifying solid shapes

Now let's see what's going on in the cave!

Sentences

Bogart sees stars that form an animal! Draw lines between the stars. Then complete the sentences with the word **see.** Write the missing letter to find out which animal he sees.

I do not see a cat.

I do not _____ a pig.

I do not _____ a rat.

I _____ a ___ish.

The stars can make pictures in the sky!

Sentences

Sam is trying to remember the things he and his friends have seen. Help Sam out. Write the word **was** to make the sentences complete.

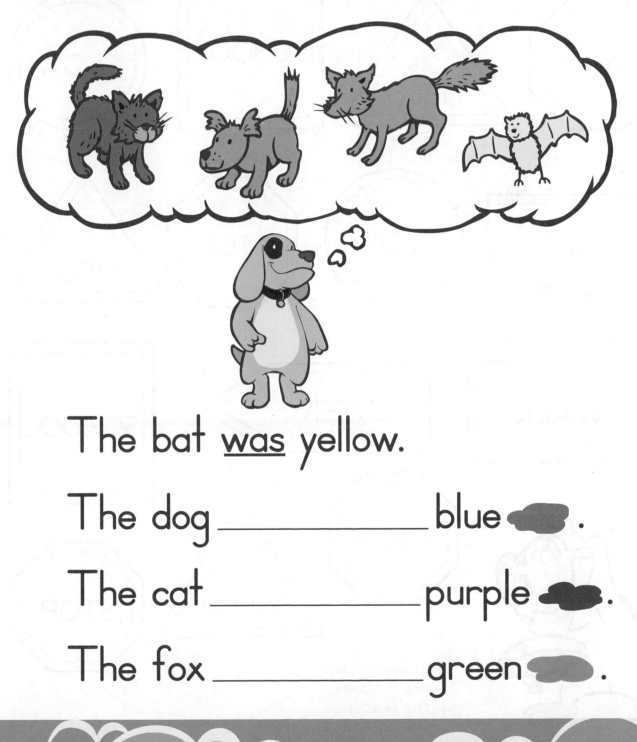

The bat <u>was</u> yellow.

The dog _____ blue.

The cat _____ purple.

The fox _____ green.

Words on Signs

Color all of the **STOP** signs you can find.

STOP

YIELD

SCHOOL

SLOW

EXIT

SLOW

STOP

YIELD

WALK

ENTER

SCHOOL

STOP

YIELD

STOP

You see those signs all over the place!

Assessment

Chapter 23 Review

Your child studied sentences, words used on signs, and three-dimensional shapes in this chapter.

Your child learned:
- Composition of simple sentences.
- Identification of traffic signs.
- Recognition of three-dimensional objects.

Work with your child on the chapter review activities shown below. If your child has difficulty with any of these exercises, go back through the chapter with him or her to review the material. You can also review and reinforce these skills with your child using the exercises in the additional activities section below.

1. Ask your child what two shapes you will find in a triangular prism.

2. How many identical rectangles are in a triangular prism? How many identical triangles are in a triangular prism?

3. Using "see" or "was," have your child complete each sentence.

I _____ the dog.
I did not _____.
He _____ happy.

Additional Activities

Here are some simple and fun things you can do with your child to practice what you have worked on in this chapter. To help reinforce what was learned in this chapter, try these activities.

1. Count how many stop signs you and your child see in a trip to the store.

2. Using index cards, make flash cards for these sight words:

SAID   DO   MY   WAS

3. Using all of the flash cards you've created for these workbook activities, have your child put together sentences. Make extra flash cards as you need them to complete sentences.

Chapter 24

Today's lesson will be lots of fun as we join Paige, Marco, and Sam while they play carnival games!

While they explore, you will have a good time learning:
• Completing sentences
• Identifying solid shapes
• Word problems

Now let's see what's going on at the carnival!

Capitalization

Read the reply Sam got from his mom. Underline each beginning word that does not start with a capital letter.

Address: Sam@space.com
Subject: Home

it is hot at home. We did not walk to the park. we rode in the van. did you get a rock on the planet? i am fine, but I miss you.
Mom

I love to get messages from Mom!

Capitalization

A sentence begins with an uppercase letter. We also call it a **capital letter.** Read Marco's e-mail message to his mom. Circle the sentences that do not begin with a capital letter.

Address: Mom@home.com

Subject: Space

We are in space. the space walk was fun. we met Zan on a planet.

how are you?

I miss you.

Marco

Finding Spheres

Find the sections that have spheres inside them. Color the sections green to find a bird that has a warm and sunny home all year long.

A sphere is a ball or a globe. A sphere looks like this:

Figuring Things Out

Making a list can help you find the answer.

Tom needs to put new 🧲 on his 🐴 He keeps his horses in three different fields. How many 🧲 does Tom need for all of his horses?

Step 1: Make a list.

Field	Number of 🐴	Number of Feet of each 🐴	Total number of Feet
North	2 horses	4 + 4	8
West	2 horses		
South	1 horse		

Step 2: A horse has ____ feet. Write a number sentence for the number of feet Tom's horses have in each field.

_____

Step 3: Add the numbers in the last column. Write the sums in the last column.

8 + ____ + ____ = ____

Tom needs to buy ____ 🧲 .

Drawing Triangular Prisms

Trace the triangular prism around each toy.

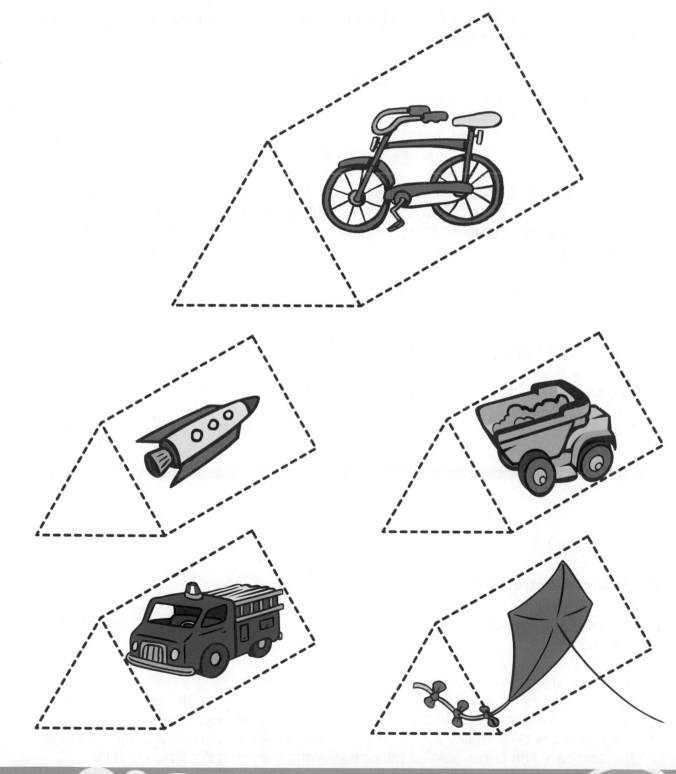

Assessment

Chapter 24 Review

In this chapter, your child studied capitalization, ending punctuation, adding combinations of numbers, and identifying shapes.

Your child learned:
- Capitalization.
- End-of-sentence punctuation.
- Addition of multiple numbers.
- Recognition of three-dimensional objects.

Do the following activities to review what your child has learned. If your child is having difficulty in any of the areas below, go back through the pages of this chapter with your child. With the additional activities listed below, you can also review and reinforce the skills covered in this chapter.

1. Ask your child to rewrite these sentences using an uppercase/capital letter to begin the sentences:

    i am happy.   we are going to the park.   are you a frog?

2. Tell your child to add the missing punctuation marks.

    The cat was yellow   What is your favorite toy   Did you go to the park

3. Have your child complete these number problems:

$$3 + 4 + 1 = \underline{\quad} \qquad 8 + 1 + 1 = \underline{\quad} \qquad 6 + 7 + 2 = \underline{\quad}$$
$$5 + 1 + 2 = \underline{\quad} \qquad 3 + 3 + 3 = \underline{\quad} \qquad 4 + 1 + 2 = \underline{\quad}$$

Additional Activities

Here are some simple and fun activities you can do with your child to practice what you have worked on in this chapter. These activities will reinforce the skills your child studied on the previous pages.

1. See how many spheres your child can find in your house.
2. Using the flash cards you have made, have your child make up sentences and have him/her point to the word that should begin with a capital, or uppercase, letter.
3. Using the index cards, make a "." and a "?" card. Give a statement or a question to your child and have him or her hold up the card showing the correct end punctuation.

Chapter 25

Today's lesson will be lots of fun as we join Marco, Quincy, and Sam while they lay on the beach!

While they explore, you will have a good time learning:
- Punctuation
- Identifying solid shapes

Now let's see what's going on at the beach!

End Punctuation

An exclamation point looks like this: !

An exclamation point goes at the end of a sentence that expresses a strong feeling. Circle the exclamation points.

That is hot !

Rosa went to the store .

This spaceship goes fast !

I am so surprised !

Who are you ?

This is so much fun !

Great job, you crazy cat!

End Punctuation

Add an exclamation point to the end of each sentence. Then write your own exclamation.

Look at that star

Ouch

What a cool planet

Watch where you are going

_____

- -

_____

Wow! You're good at this!

Drawing Spheres

Help these kids make water balloons.
Trace over each sphere you see.

Now we're ready for some action!

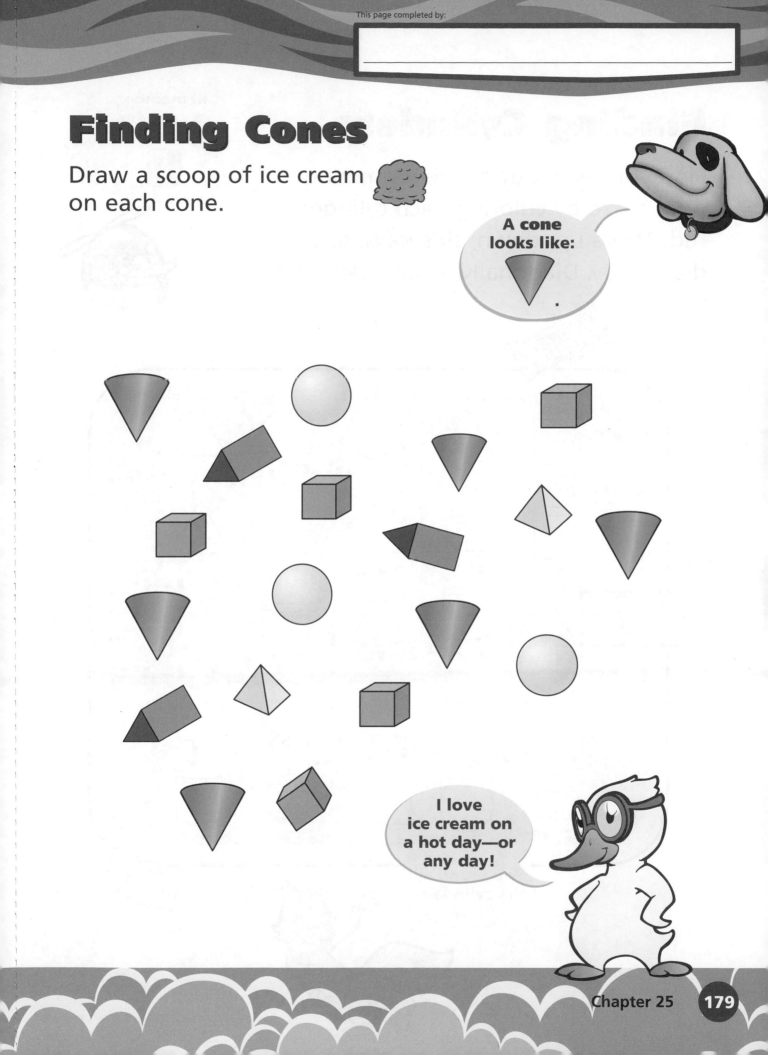

Finding Cones

Draw a scoop of ice cream on each cone.

A cone looks like:

I love ice cream on a hot day—or any day!

Finding Cylinders

Find your way out of the swimming pool maze by coloring each cylinder red. Move up, down, sideways, and diagonally. Diagonally means slantwise.

Remember, a cylinder looks like:

Start

You found all the cylinders!

Assessment

Chapter 25 Review

In this chapter, your child studied ending punctuation, drawing spheres and cones, and identifying cylinders.

Your child learned:
- End-of-sentence punctuation.
- Recognition of three-dimensional objects.

To review what your child has learned, do the 3 activities below. If your child is having difficulty in any of the areas below, go back and review the pages with him or her. You can also review and reinforce the skills in this section with the additional activities listed below.

1. Ask your child what punctuation he/she would use at the end of these sentences.

   I love you   How are you   I'm sleepy   What time is it

2. Ask your child, "When do you use an exclamation point at the end of a sentence?"

3. Have your child draw a sphere, a cone, and a cylinder. Using just those shapes, see if your child can make a drawing of a person.

Additional Activities

Here are some simple and fun activities you can do with your child to practice what you have worked on in Chapter 25. These activities will reinforce the skills your child learned on the previous pages.

1. Have your child think about the different shapes of food. Play a guessing game where you and your child take turns giving clues for mystery foods. The only descriptors you can use are shapes and colors. (Example: a white sphere with a brown cone describes an ice cream cone.)
2. Ask your child to tell you how letters of the alphabet resemble different shapes.
3. Save the empty cardboard cylinders from paper towels and toilet paper and have your child use his or her imagination to build whatever he or she wants.

Chapter 26

Today's lesson will be lots of fun as we join Rosa and Bogart while they visit the zoo!

While they explore, you will have a good time learning:
- Completing sentences
- Identifying solid shapes
- Word problems

Now let's see what's going on at the zoo!

Sentences

Read each group of words below.
Circle the sentences.

We will fly in space.

Sam has a space hat.

went to

We will go in a.

Sam

I like to be in space.

We will go in a *what?*

A sentence is a group of words that work together to make a complete thought.

Sentences

Read each group of words below. Cross out the ones that are not complete sentences.

We will go in a spaceship.

Will fly.

Is big.

The spaceship is big.

In a spaceship.

You can go.

Do you have a spaceship?

Have a spaceship.

Not all sentences are long. **You can go** is a short sentence, but it is a complete thought!

Sentences

Read the words in the stars. If the words make a complete sentence, color the star.

We are up in the sky.

We are

in the sky.

Can go to a star.

We can go to a star!

A star is in the sky.

Drawing Cylinders

Lemonade is great on a hot day.
Trace each cylinder you see.

This makes me thirsty!

Figuring Things Out

Marco wants to play with his ball on the top shelf. Which object is safest to stand on to reach the ball?

Marco's choices are a cylinder, a cone, a sphere, and a cube.

Should he use a cylinder? _____

Why or why not? _____

_____

_____

Should he use a cone? _____

Why or why not? _____

_____

_____

Should he use a sphere? _____

Why or why not? _____

_____

_____

Should he use a cube? _____

Why or why not? _____

_____

Assessment

Chapter 26 Review

In this chapter, your child studied sentences, three-dimensional shapes, and objective thinking.

Your child learned:
- Recognition of complete sentences.
- Identification of three-dimensional shapes.
- Comprehension of information.

To review what your child has learned, do the 3 activities below. If your child is having difficulty in any of the areas below, go back and review the pages with him or her. You can also review and reinforce the skills in this section with the additional activities listed below.

1. In the pictures below, ask your child to color the cones red and color the spheres blue.

2. On a separate piece of paper, help your child write a full sentence about the color of the spaceship below.

3. Have your child circle the cone shapes in the pictures below.

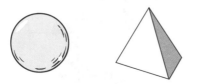  

Additional Activities
Here are some simple and fun activities you can do with your child to practice what you have worked on in this chapter. These activities will reinforce the skills your child studied on the previous pages.

1. While reading a storybook, have your child count the number of sentences on the page.
2. Throughout your home, have your child find spheres, cones, cubes, and cylinders in everyday objects or toys.
3. Using the found objects from the activity above, discuss which shapes would be best for building a house.

Chapter 27

Today's lesson will be lots of fun as we join Rosa, Sam, and Bogart at the zoo!

While they explore, you will have a good time learning:
• Completing sentences
• Identifying solid shapes

Now let's see what's going on at the zoo!

27

Sentences

Write a word from a star to make each group of words a complete sentence.

space

star

sky

We are in _____ .

I see a _____ !

It is in the _____ .

You're good at completing sentences!

Sentences

When you put the words together, you have sentences!

Look at the picture.
Then draw lines to match the words in **Box A**
with the words in **Box B** to make sentences!

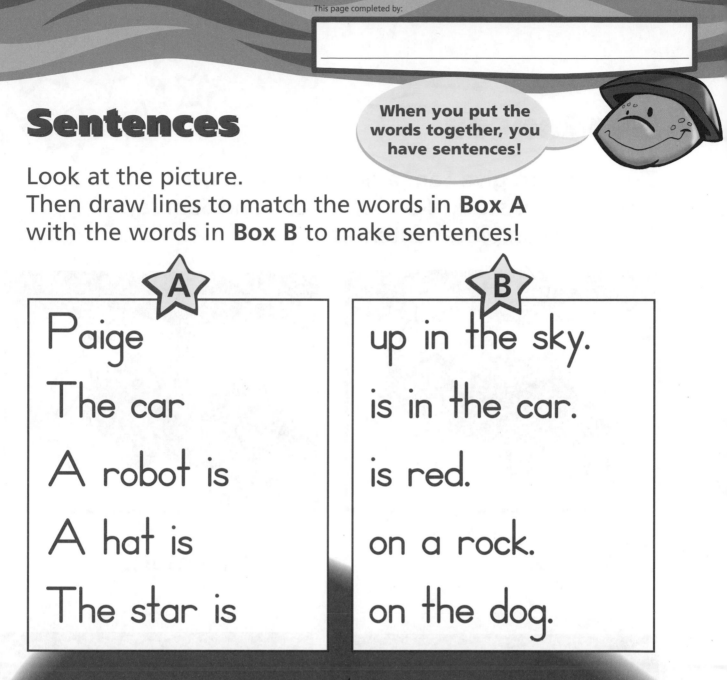

A

Paige

The car

A robot is

A hat is

The star is

B

up in the sky.

is in the car.

is red.

on a rock.

on the dog.

This page completed by:

Sentences

Zan wants to give Sam a ride in his Min car.
But the car is stuck! Read what Zan and Sam say.
Circle the complete sentences.

Not go.

I can push.

Min car not.

We can walk!

Sentences

There are words in the stars! On the lines below, write a sentence with the words. Put them in an order that makes sense. Start with the word **The.**

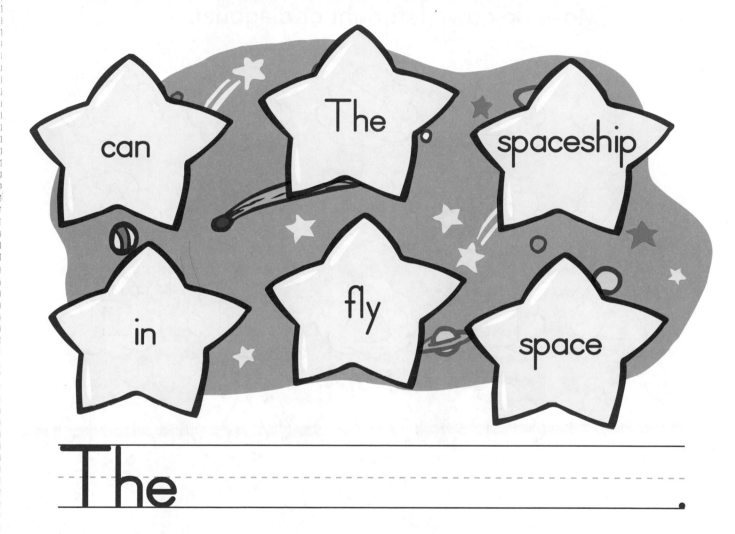

The _____ .

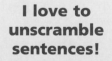
I love to unscramble sentences!

Finding Solids

Help Rosa find her way out of the maze by coloring the following solids in order: a cube, then a cylinder, then a sphere, then a cube, then a cylinder, and last a sphere. Move up, down, left, right or diagonal.

Start

Cloud hopping is fun!

End

Assessment

Chapter 27 Review

In this chapter, your child studied sentences, three-dimensional shapes, and objective thinking.

Your child learned:
- Recognition of complete sentences.
- Identification of three-dimensional shapes.

To review what your child has learned, do the 2 activities below. If your child is having difficulty in any of the areas below, go back and review the pages with him or her. You can also review and reinforce the skills in this section with the additional activities listed below.

1. Have your child finish the sentence below using the picture.

Paige is _____.

2. Have your child circle the row below that shows the pattern cube, cylinder, sphere, cube, cylinder, sphere.

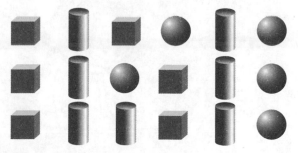

Additional Activities

Here are some simple and fun activities you can do with your child to practice what you have worked on in Chapter 27. These activities will reinforce the skills your child learned on the previous pages.

1. Choose a picture from a favorite story book and help your child write complete sentences that describe the picture.
2. While unloading the groceries from the store, have your child identify spheres, cones, cubes, and cylinders.
3. Make a pattern on the sidewalk with chalk using cubes, cylinders, spheres, and cones. Call out shapes for your child to hop to.

Chapter 28

Today's lesson will be lots of fun as we join Bogart and Rosa piloting a flying saucer throughout the solar system!

While they explore, you will have a good time learning:
• Nouns
• Sorting solids

Now let's see what's going on in outer space!

Sentences

Help Paige unscramble some more sentences. Write the sentence below each group of words. Put the words in an order that makes sense.

I space in am.

_____

in am spaceship I the.

_____

I moon see the.

_____

Those sentences didn't make sense until you unscrambled them!

Sentences

Marco found a space rock for his collection. Look at the pictures and read the words next to them. Do the words make sense? Write **in** or **out** on the lines. Now do the sentences make sense?

The rock was _____ the bag.

It was _____ of the bag.

It was _____ the box.

It was _____ of the box.

I like being **in** a spaceship. But maybe it's time to go **out** for a walk!

Sentences

Marco and Sam are going for a space walk! Let's listen to what they are saying. Draw lines to match the words in **Cloud A** with the words in **Cloud B.**

A

The sky

I can

The moon is

We are out of

B

the spaceship.

see the moon.

is blue.

big and yellow.

Say the sentences you made. Do they make sense?

Finding Named Shapes

Find the named shapes.

Color each section with a cone inside yellow.
Color each section with a pyramid inside blue.
Color each section with a triangular prism inside red.

What a pretty ball!

Matching Solids to Their Names

Draw a line from the picture of each solid to its name.

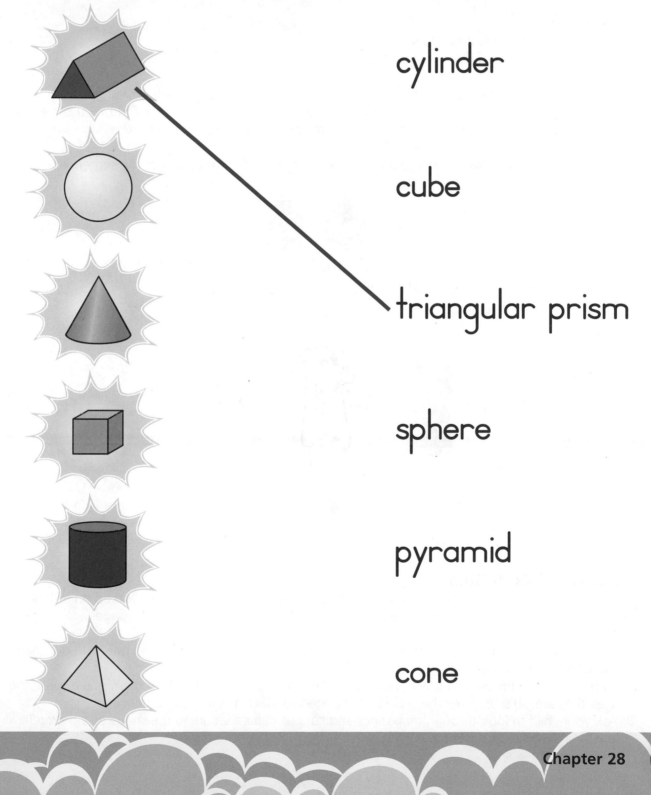

cylinder

cube

triangular prism

sphere

pyramid

cone

Assessment

Chapter 28 Review

Your child studied complete sentences and three-dimensional shapes in this chapter.

Your child learned:
- Recognition of complete sentences.
- Identification of three-dimensional shapes.

Do the following activities to review what your child has learned. If your child is having difficulty in any of the areas below, go back through the pages of this chapter with your child. You can also review and reinforce the skills in this section with the additional activities listed below.

1. In the blank space provided, tell your child to write the words that complete the sentence:

The _____ are _____ and yellow.

2. Using the picture, have your child complete the following sentences:

The _____ is above Sam.
The _____ is below Sam.
The cylinder is to the _____ of Sam.

Additional Activities
Here are some interactive ways you and your child can practice what you have worked on in this chapter. These activities will reinforce the skills your child studied on the previous pages.

1. Find simple sentences in the newspaper. Cut the words apart and then have your child put them back together in order.
2. Look at street signs around town. Discuss whether or not the sentences on them make sense the way they are. Discuss how they could be changed to make a complete sentence.
3. Ask your child to look through magazines and cut out items that are in the shape of a triangular prism, a pyramid, and a cone.

Chapter 29

Today's lesson will be lots of fun as we join Marco as he swims in the deep blue see!

While he explores, you will have a good time learning:
- Capitalization
- Comprehension
- Identifying solid shapes

Now let's see what's going on under the sea!

Capitalization

Look at the picture. Then write a word to begin each sentence. The words you need are in the star. Remember to begin with a capital letter!

we   my   is

_____ are on planet Yum.

_____ a dog on the planet?

_____ apple is yummy!

Great work!

Answering Questions

Paige sees a monkey in the jungle! Look at the pictures. Then use three of the words from the box to answer the question below.

walk   write   climb   swing   read

What can the monkey do?

It can _____ .

It can _____

It can _____

Good work!

Answering Questions

Look at the pictures. Then answer each question.
Use words from the box in your answers.

monkey	tiger	parrot	snake	elephant

 I see an animal with stripes!
What is it? It is a _____ .

 I see an animal with feathers!
What is it? It is a _____ .

 I see a big gray animal.
What is it? It is an _____ .

Describing Combined Solids

Name the two solids that make up each figure.

_____

_____

_____

_____

That was great!

Identifying Similar Solids

Draw a line between the solids that are alike but have different sizes.

Similar objects are shaped alike.

You really know your shapes!

Assessment

Chapter 29 Review

In this chapter, your child studied capitalization of letters, answering questions, and identifying and describing three-dimensional shapes.

Your child learned:
- Capitalization of words.
- Recognition of three-dimensional shapes.
- Verbalization of observed objects.

Work with your child on the chapter review activities shown below. If your child has difficulty with any of these exercises, go back through the chapter with him or her to review the material. You can also review and reinforce these skills with your child using the exercises in the additional activities section below.

1. Have your child change the first word in each sentence to make it correct:

> an lion ate an apple.
> we dog was on the planet.
> the were on planet yum.

2. Ask your child to look at the picture and answer each question:

Which animal is the biggest? _____

Which animal is next to the tiger? _____

Which animals are under the monkey? _____ and _____

Additional Activities

Here are some simple and fun things you can do with your child to practice what you have worked on in this chapter. To help reinforce what was learned in this chapter, try these activities.

1. While reading a story book, ask your child to describe what the characters are doing in each picture.
2. You and your child can make a snack mix using foods of different shapes such as cones, spheres, and cylinders.
3. While looking at a magazine or newspaper, have your child draw circles around capital letters.

Chapter 30

Today's lesson will be lots of fun as we join Quincy, Rosa, and friends as they play in their treehouse!

While they explore, you will have a good time learning:
- Nouns
- Sorting solids

Now let's see what's going on in the treehouse!

Naming Words: Places

Marco is daydreaming about home. Some words name a place. The word **desert** names a place. Circle each word in Marco's daydream that names a place.

home

bike

school

kite

park

store

P. Jones©

Naming Words: Places

Read the postcard Sam wrote to a friend at school.
Underline the words that name places.

Dear Peg,
I am in the desert.
It is not a garden.
It is not a beach.
But it is fun!

Sam

Peg
Sunshine
School

I like keeping in touch with my friends!

Naming Words

Rosa shows Sam some pictures from home. Underline the words that name people. Circle the words that name places.

a boy in school

the library

my teacher

the park

I love school!

Sorting by Shape

Draw lines to connect solids that are the same.
Use an orange line to connect cones. Use a purple
line to connect triangular prisms. Use a green
line to connect cubes. Use a red line to
connect cylinders.

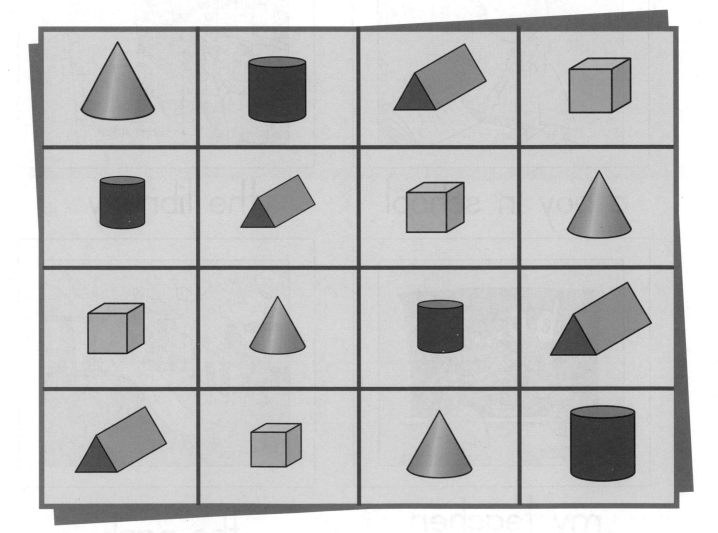

Reasoning Skills

Which solid is Quincy thinking about?

Quincy is NOT thinking about the solid that has square faces.

Quincy is NOT thinking about the solid that has a circular top and bottom.

Quincy is NOT thinking about the solid that is shaped like a beach ball.

Quincy is NOT thinking about the solid that has one circular bottom.

Draw an *X* over the solids Quincy is **NOT** thinking about. Only one solid will remain when you are finished.

Which solid is Quincy thinking about? _____

Identifying Congruent Solids

Using four different colors, color all of the congruent solids the same color.

Congruent solids have the same size and shape.

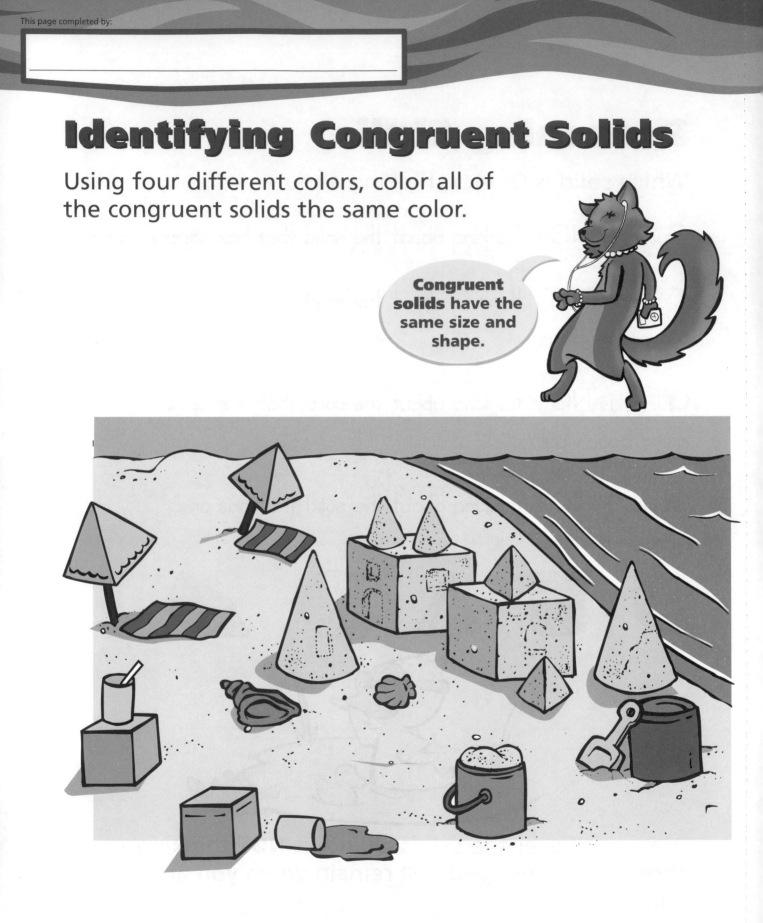

Assessment

Chapter 30 Review

In this chapter, your child studied understanding word meanings and distinguishing shapes.

Your child learned:
- Comprehension of words.
- Recognition of differences among three-dimensional shapes.
- Identification of congruent solids.

To review what your child has learned, do the 2 activities below. If your child is having difficulty in any of the areas below, go back and review the pages with him or her. You can also review and reinforce the skills in this section with the additional activities listed below.

1. Have your child circle the word in each group that names a place:

a.	rock	kite	home	bike
b.	sand	fish	beach	shell
c.	apple	store	gum	sandwich

2. Direct your child to underline the words that name the person in each sentence:

My teacher is at school.
My friend was at the park.
The lifeguard was at the beach.

Additional Activities
Below are some interactive ways you and your child can practice what you have worked on in this chapter. These activities will reinforce the skills your child studied on the previous pages.

1. Help your child send a postcard to a friend and write a sentence on it using a word that names a place.
2. Ask your child to find toys that are the shapes of the solids on page 214. Sort the different shapes into separate piles.
3. Do the following activity with your child:
   Around your home, find containers that are the same shapes as the shapes on page 214. Fill them with water and freeze them in the freezer. When they are frozen, take them outside and build with them.

Chapter 31

Today's lesson will be lots of fun as we join Rosa and Quincy exploring an iceberg!

While they explore, you will have a good time learning:
- Comprehension
- Verbs
- Word problems

Now let's have an Antarctic adventure!

Naming Words: Things

Some words name things. The word **plant** names a thing. So does the word **owl.** Look at the desert animals below. Draw lines to match the animals to the names in the box.

bat   lizard   snake   fox

Some more words that name things are **ball, popcorn, and tree.**

Naming Words: Things

Paige and Sam are playing a guessing game. Sam gives clues to Paige. Help Paige guess what Sam is thinking about. Then write the answer on the line.

It is not red.   Is it a van?

It is not big.   Is it a top?

I have it on.   It is a _____ !

You're doing
a great job!

Naming Words

Help Paige sort her word cards. Decide which words name people, which name places, and which name things. Draw a line from each picture to the box where it belongs.

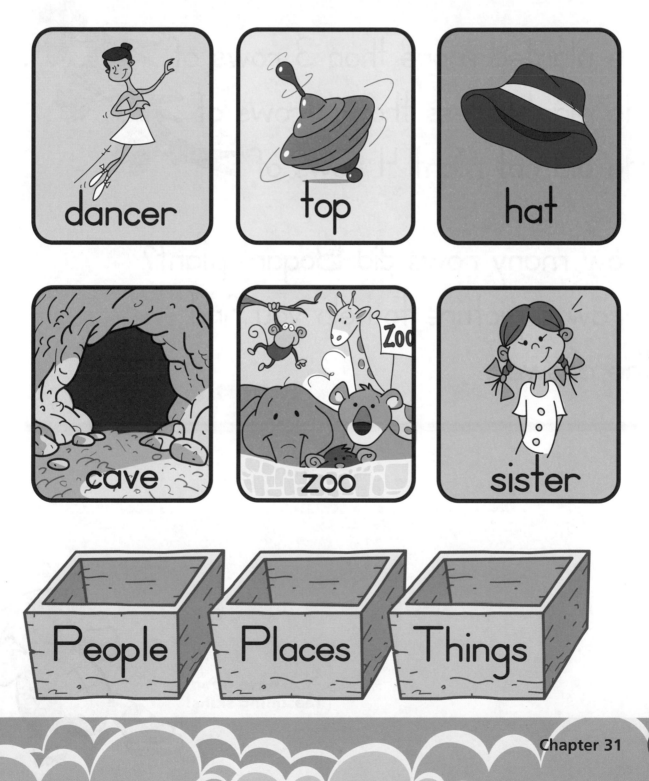

Thinking Things Through

How many rows of 🥕 did Bogart plant?

He planted more than 3 rows of 🥕.
He planted less than 6 rows of 🥕.
He did not plant 4 rows of 🥕.

How many rows did Bogart plant?
Draw a picture to help you find
the answer.

You have good
reasoning skills!

Talking About Things

Play this game with a friend.

Step 1: Your friend picks a number between 1 and 50. _____

Step 2: You pick a different number between 1 and 50. _____

Step 3: Choose a third number between your friend's number
and your number. _____

Each of you makes
a chart on a sheet
of paper. It should
look like this.

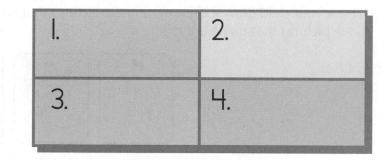

Have an adult read the following instructions for each
square. See who can do each one first correctly.

Square 1: From the three numbers, write the one
closest to 45.

Square 2: Write the number that comes after the
largest number of the three numbers.

Square 3: Draw base 10 blocks to show
the smallest number.

Square 4: Write all three
numbers in order
from smallest to largest,
and show all of the numbers
in between the three numbers.

Assessment

Chapter 31 Review

In Chapter 31, your child studied understanding word meanings, solving problems, and reasoning.

Your child learned:
- Comprehension of words.
- Problem solving through deductive reasoning.
- Differentiation of word meanings.

To review what your child has learned, do the activities below. Review the pages of this chapter with your child if he or she if is having difficulty in any of the areas below. You can also review and reinforce the skills in this section with the additional activities listed below.

1. Have your child draw a circle around the pictures that name a place, and draw a line under the pictures that name a thing.

2. Have your child use a separate sheet of paper to draw a picture to help you find the answer to this question: Marco collected 8 heads of lettuce. Marco lost 3 of the heads of lettuce. How many heads of lettuce did Marco have left?

3. Tell your child to use the following numbers to answer some questions:

34   43   47   28   37

Which number is the smallest?
Which number is the closest to 50?
Which number comes between 28 and 37?

Additional Activities

Here are some simple and fun activities you can do with your child to practice what you have worked on in this chapter. These activities will reinforce the skills your child studied on the previous pages.

1. Go on a walk and have your child name five places and five things that are seen along the way.
2. Choose a thing in your home. Give your child clues about the thing until your child can guess what the thing is.
3. Cut numbers out of a newspaper or magazine. Have your child answer questions about the numbers.
   Which is the largest? Which is the smallest? Are any of the numbers the same?

Chapter 32

Today's lesson will be lots of fun as we join Bogart sledding down a hill!

While he explores, you will have a good time learning:
- Comprehension
- Verbs
- Word problems

Now let's have a Winter adventure!

Naming Words: Actions

Words like **hop, throw,** and **crawl** name actions, or things you can do! Draw lines to match the words in the box to the pictures of what Paige is doing.

sit   jump   draw   nap

An action word I like is **sing.**

Word Meanings

Write the word from the box that goes with each picture.

I like to do all of those things! Do you?

run   hop   swim   dance

Finding Pyramids

Circle the pyramid in each set.

A pyramid looks like: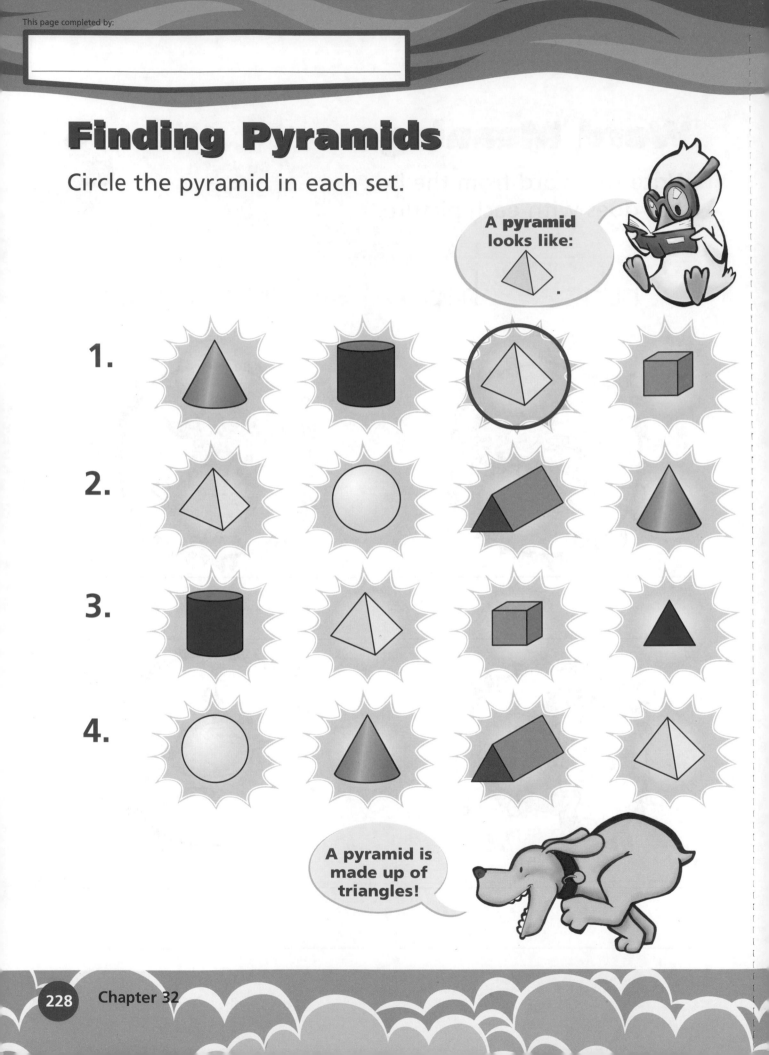

1.

2.

3.

4.

A pyramid is made up of triangles!

Reasoning Skills

Which solid is Sam thinking about?

Sam is NOT thinking about the solid that has square faces.

Sam is NOT thinking about the solid that has a circular top and bottom.

Sam is NOT thinking about the solid that is shaped like a beach ball.

Sam is NOT thinking about the solid that has one circular bottom.

Draw an *X* over the solids Sam is **NOT** thinking about. Only one solid will remain when you are finished.

Which solid is Sam thinking about? _____

Thinking Things Through

Joe has 🐤 , 🐎 , and 🐑 on his farm.

He has more 🐤 than he has 🐑 and 🐎 .

He has more 🐑 than 🐎 .

Circle the animal which Joe has fewer of than any other animal.

Good thinking!

Assessment

Chapter 32 Review

In this chapter, you and your child studied understanding word meanings as well as reasoning and understanding.

Your child learned:
- Comprehension of words.
- Identification of action words.
- Problem solving through deductive reasoning.

Do the following activities to review what your child has learned. If your child is having difficulty in any of the areas below, go back through the pages of this chapter with your child. With the additional activities listed below, you can also review and reinforce the skills covered in this chapter.

1. Have your child draw a line to connect each picture with an action word.

Swimming

Hopping

Running

2. Tell your child to draw a line to connect each picture with an action word.

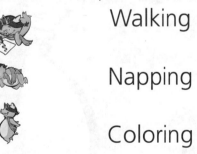

Walking

Napping

Coloring

Additional Activities
Here are some simple and fun things you can do with your child to practice what you have worked on in this chapter. To help reinforce what was learned in this chapter, try these activities.

1. Write a few action words on different pieces of paper. Have your child pick one and act it out.
2. While reading a story, choose a picture in a book and have your child describe the action in the picture.

Chapter 33

Today's lesson will be lots of fun as we join Sam and Paige splashing in the pool!

As we play, you will have a good time learning:
- Verbs
- Word problems

Now let's see what's going on in the pool!

Naming Words: Actions

Look at the pictures. Then circle each word that names an action.

dig

station

pull

draw

piano

ride

Naming Words: Actions

Draw a picture of something you would like to do when you grow up. Write an action word under your picture.

I'd like to fly into space!

Matching Parts of a Group

Quincy has played all day. Now it's snack time!

Circle the fraction that represents the number of ice cream cones that are vanilla.

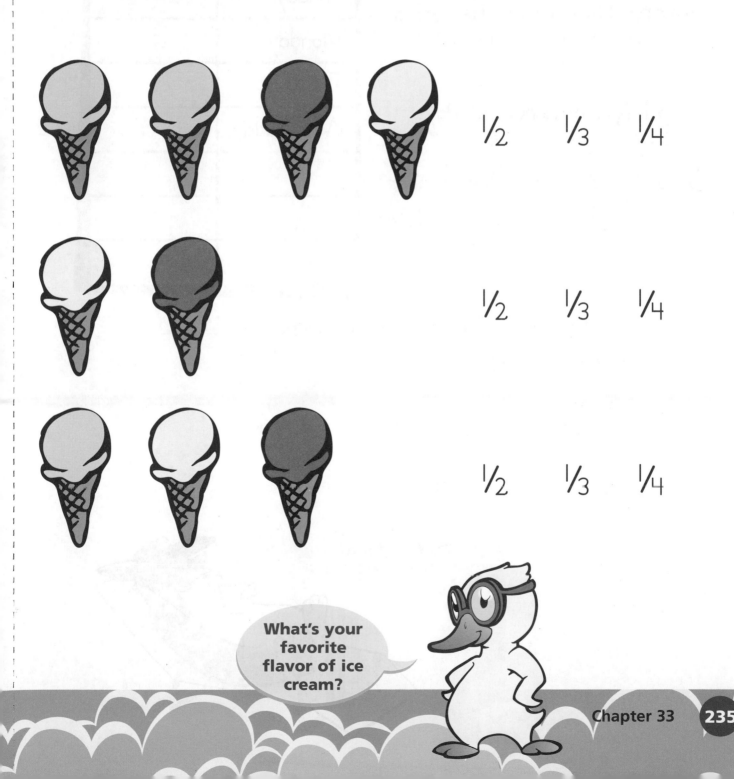

½ ⅓ ¼

½ ⅓ ¼

½ ⅓ ¼

What's your favorite flavor of ice cream?

Figuring Things Out

Marco the Penguin ate two bananas on Sunday. Then each day, he ate two more bananas than he did the day before. How many bananas did he eat on Saturday?

Day	Bananas eaten
Sunday	2
Monday	
Tuesday	
Wednesday	

Step 1: Make a chart of days.

Step 2: Add to find the number of bananas Marco ate on Monday.

How many bananas did Marco eat on Sunday? _____
How many on Monday? _____

Step 3: Continue adding until the chart is filled.

Marco ate _____ bananas on Saturday.

That's a lot of bananas!

Modeling Problems

Draw a line from each set of pictures to its description.

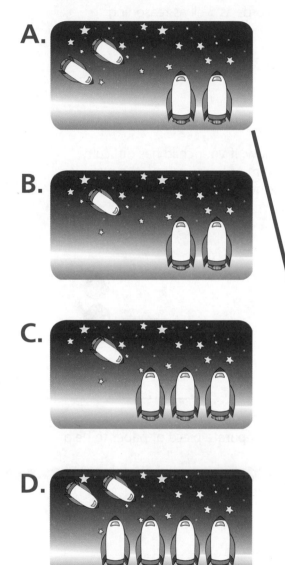

1. Two rockets are on the ground. One rocket is coming in for a landing. There will be three rockets total on the ground.

2. Four rockets are on the ground. Two rockets are coming in for a landing. There will be six rockets total on the ground.

3. Three rockets are on the ground. One rocket is coming in for a landing. There will be four rockets total on the ground.

4. Two rockets are on the ground. Two rockets are coming in for a landing. There will be four rockets total on the ground.

Would you like to be an astronaut when you grow up?

Assessment

Chapter 33 Review

In this chapter, you and your child studied naming and action words as well as reasoning and problem solving.

Your child learned:
- Identification of naming words.
- Identification of action words.
- Problem solving through deductive reasoning.

Work with your child on the chapter review activities shown below. If your child has difficulty with any of these exercises, go back through the chapter with him or her to review the material. You can also review and reinforce these skills with your child using the exercises in the additional activities section below.

1. Have your child write the action word under each picture;

_____   _____   _____

2. Quincy's garden is really growing! Have your child draw on a separate piece of paper to help you solve the problem:

   On the first day, two carrots grew.
   On the second day, three more carrots grew.
   On the third day, two more carrots grew.
   How many carrots are in Quincy's garden?

Additional Activities
Below are some interactive ways you and your child can review what you have worked on in this chapter. These activities will reinforce the skills your child studied on the previous pages.

1. Have your child draw a picture of some of the actions that he/she has done today.
2. Using toys, ask your child to make up a story in which there are a few toys, and then other toys are added to the group. Have your child use the toys to demonstrate the story.
3. While eating a snack mix that has 15 pieces, have your child eat 2 pieces and then count the remaining pieces. Have your child eat three more pieces and count what is left. Continue with different pieces until the snack is gone.

Chapter 34

Today's lesson will be lots of fun as we join Quincy and Rosa in their playhouse!

While they explore, you will have a good time learning:
- Verbs
- Word problems

Now let's see what's going on in the playhouse!

Naming Words: Actions

Write each action word where it belongs.

sing   dance   swim   k<u>ic</u>k

Nice job!

Naming Words: Actions

Marco has a riddle for Quincy. See if you can answer the riddle with a word from the box. Write the word on the line. Then circle the action words.

worm   bird   fish   fox

It cannot climb.

It can swim.

It cannot fly.

It is a

_____

Can you think of a riddle with action words in it?

Naming Words: Actions

Draw and write about the things you like to do.

You can do anything!

Modeling Problems

Draw a line from each set of pictures to its description.

A.

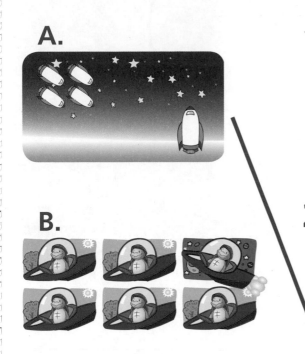

1. Three rockets are on the ground. Four rockets are coming in for a landing. There will be seven rockets total on the ground.

B.

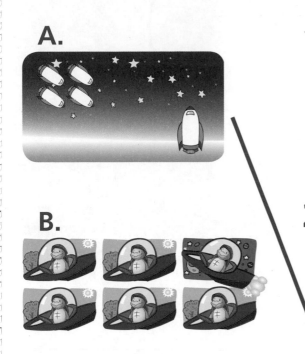

2. Six astronauts are waiting to take off. One astronaut takes off. There are five astronauts waiting to take off.

C.

3. One rocket is on the ground. Four rockets are coming in for a landing. There will be five rockets total on the ground.

D.

4. Two rockets are on the ground. Three rockets are coming in for a landing. There will be five rockets total on the ground.

Thinking Things Through

好奇，线索   想出 第步 理解

Use the clues to figure out
how many moons Jupiter has.

木星

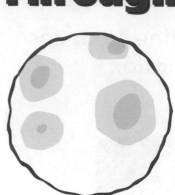

Jupiter has more than 12 moons.

Jupiter has fewer than 18 moons.

Draw a picture of the possible moons
Jupiter has, and number them.

12 14 16 18

X   ✓

偶数

Jupiter has an even number of moons. Draw a picture
of the possible moons Jupiter has, and number them.

Jupiter does not have only 14 moons.
Therefore, Jupiter has ___16___ moons.

Assessment

Chapter 34 Review

Your child studied naming and action words as well as reasoning and problem solving in this chapter.

Your child learned:
- Identification of naming words.
- Identification of action words.
- Problem solving through observation.
- Problem solving through modeling.

Do the following activities to review what your child has learned. If your child is having difficulty in any of the areas below, go back through the pages of this chapter with your child. With the additional activities listed below, you can also review and reinforce the skills covered in this chapter.

1. Tell your child to use the clues to decide the answer and to circle the correct picture.
   It cannot fly. It doesn't have fins. It can talk.

2. Tell your child to use the following clues to figure out how many rockets took off:

    11 13 15

              There were more then 10 rockets.
              There were fewer then 16 rockets.
              The number of rockets that took off was not an even number.
              The number of takeoffs was less than 13.
              How many rockets took off?

Additional Activities

Below are some interactive ways you and your child can review what you have worked on in this chapter. These activities will reinforce the skills your child studied on the previous pages.

1. Perform an action for your child. Have your child write the action word on a piece of paper.
2. While unloading the groceries, make up a story to tell your child what item and how many of them to put away. (For example: Start with 5 cans of soup. Say "First, put away two cans of soup. How many cans of soup are left?")
3. Use pennies and dimes. Give your child directions about which coins to add to a pile in order to gather the number of coins you are thinking about.

Chapter 35

Today's lesson will be lots of fun as we join Marco and Bogart floating deep in outer space!

While they explore, you will have a good time learning:
• Verbs
• Completing sentences
• Graphing
• Sequencing

Now let's see what's going on in outer space!

Repeating and Extending Patterns

Continue the pattern by drawing its parts in the spaces below.

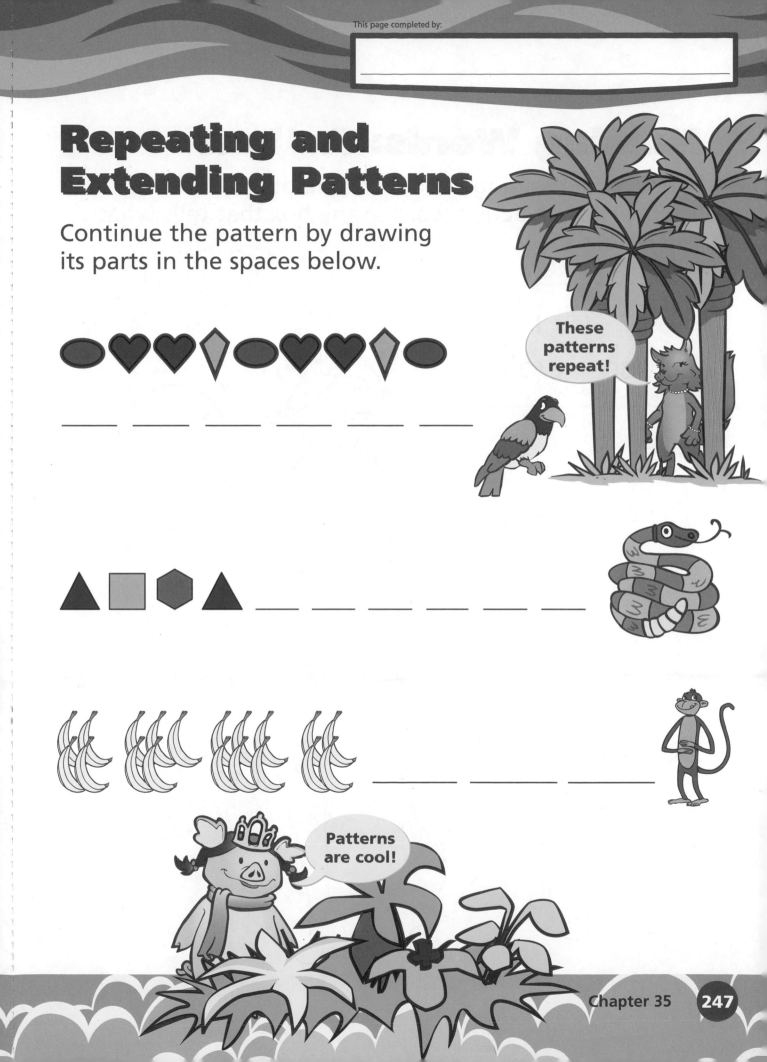

These patterns repeat!

Patterns are cool!

This page completed by:

Naming Words: Actions

What is Paige doing? Connect the dots to find out.
Then circle the action word in the box that tells what
she is doing.

eat   ride
brush walk

Sentences

Draw a picture of a robot. Then complete the sentences to tell what your robot can do. Choose words from the box or think of other words.

jump	eat	run
walk	talk	hop

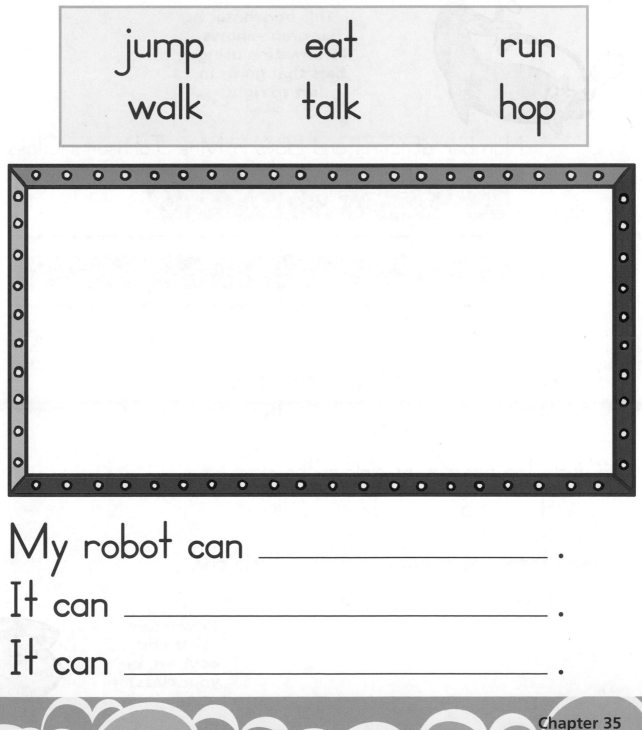

My robot can _____.

It can _____.

It can _____.

Reading a Horizontal Bar Graph

Look at this bar graph of Mrs. Johnson's class.

This horizontal bar graph shows information using bars that go from left to right.

Number of Girls and Boys in Mrs. Johnson's Class

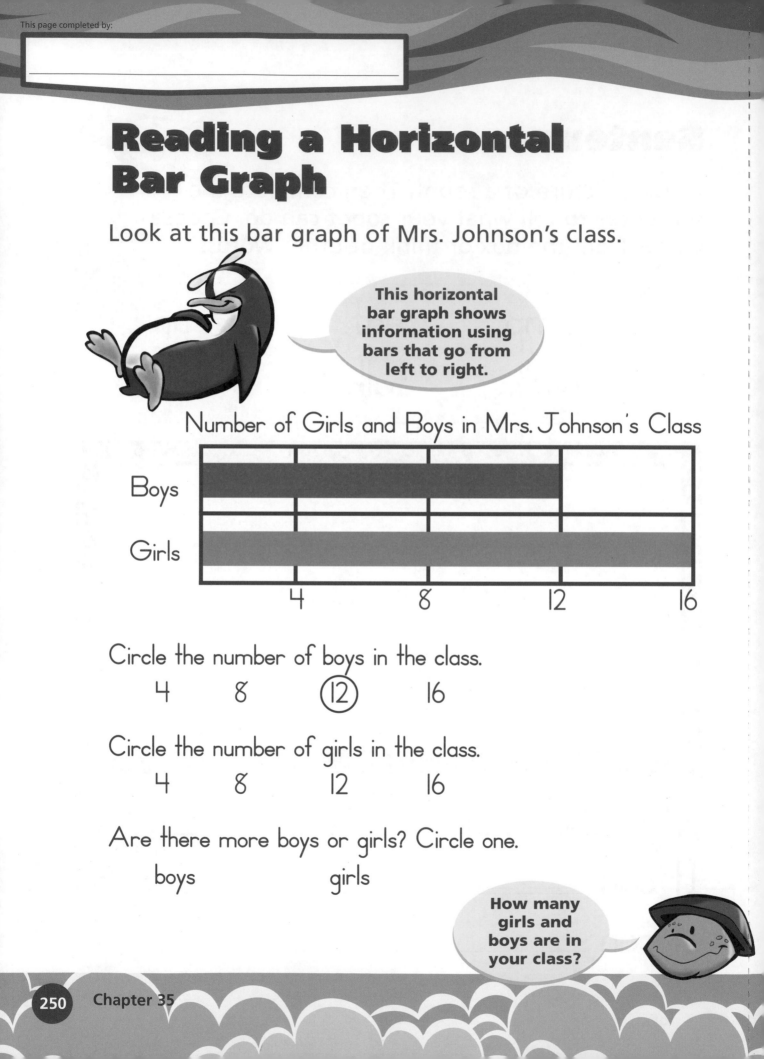

Circle the number of boys in the class.

4   8   (12)   16

Circle the number of girls in the class.

4   8   12   16

Are there more boys or girls? Circle one.

boys   girls

How many girls and boys are in your class?

Identifying What Happens First

Circle the event in each set that happens **first**.

Nice work!

Assessment

Chapter 35 Review

In this chapter, your child studied recognizing action words, composing sentences, reading graphs, and understanding the order of events.

Your child learned:
- Identification of action words.
- Composition of sentences.
- Interpretation of graphs.
- Recognition of sequential events.

Do the following activities to review what your child has learned. If your child is having difficulty in any of the areas below, go back through the pages of this chapter with your child. You can also review and reinforce the skills in this section with the additional activities listed below.

1. Explain to your child that there are four things Andrew does to start his day. Have your child read each sentence and then circle the sentence that tells what would come first. Underline the sentence that would come last.

   Andrew eats breakfast.
   Andrew wakes up.
   Andrew leaves for school.
   Andrew brushes his teeth.

2. Have your child fill in the graph with the correct numbers using this information:
   Sam ate four carrots on Wednesday. He ate six carrots on Thursday.

Number of carrots Sam ate on Wednesday and Thursday					
Wednesday					
Thursday					

   0   2   4   6   8   10

3. Tell your child to use the above graph and write the day that Sam ate more carrots.

_____

Additional Activities

Below are some interactive ways you and your child can practice what you have worked on in this chapter. These activities will reinforce the skills your child studied on the previous pages.

1. Find pennies and nickels around the house. Put the pennies in one row and nickels in another row. Discuss the results.
2. Ask your child to write the action words for three things he or she does before going to school. As you fix dinner, take out different items and discuss what must happen to them first before you can eat them.

Chapter 36

Today's lesson will be lots of fun as we join Marco and Paige in the jungle!

While they explore, you'll have a good time learning:
- Comprehension
- Verbs
- Time by the hour and half hour

Now let's see what's going on in the jungle!

Word Meanings

For each pair of sentences, draw a picture of what Sam and Marco see!

"A <u>blue flower!</u>"
said Sam.
"A <u>red flower!</u>"
said Marco.

"A <u>big frog!</u>"
said Sam.
"And a <u>small fly!</u>"
said Marco.

Naming Words

Sam is making a list of things he will do when he goes home. Circle each word that names an action. Underline each word that names a thing.

(climb) a tree

(kick) a ball

ride my (bike)

(run) on the grass

Naming Words

Read what the people are saying. Circle each word that names an action. Underline each word that names a person. Draw a box around each word that names a place.

 The desert is hot.

 Let's walk to the park.

 Can we play with the baby?

 Can we eat?

Figuring Things Out

To count on, you add a number to each number you count.

Quincy has a  in his flower garden.

At 1:00 he saw 2 at the .

At 2:30 he saw 3 more at the .

At 5:00 he saw 1 more at the .

How many did Quincy see at the .

Step 1: Draw a picture for 1:00.

Step 2: Draw the birds for 2:30.

Step 3: Draw the birds for 5:00.

Step 4: Count the birds that you drew.
Quincy saw _____ .

Great job!

Reading Clocks on the Half Hour

Using 3 different colors, color the clock faces that show the same time with the same color.

These clocks read half past the hour!

Assessment

Chapter 36 Review

In this chapter, your child studied descriptive words, telling time, and problem solving.

Your child learned:
- Recognition of descriptive words.
- Reading clocks; telling time.
- Interpretation of visual and written information.

The following activities will provide a review of what your child has learned. If he or she has any difficulty in any of the areas below, go back through the pages of this chapter with your child. You can also review and reinforce the skills in this section with the additional activities listed below.

1. Ask your child to write the action words that he or she circled earlier in chapter 36. Then, have them think up four more action words and write them down.

2. The birds like to eat the worms in Joe's garden. Tell your child to read the sentences and then write the number of birds that ate worms in Joe's garden.

> At 8:00, 3 birds ate worms in Joe's garden.
> At 9:30, 2 birds ate worms in Joe's garden.
> At 11:30, Joe saw 4 more birds eating worms in his garden.

How many birds ate worms from Joe's garden?

Additional Activities

Below are some interactive ways you and your child can review what you have worked on in this chapter. These activities will reinforce the skills your child studied on the previous pages.

1. Look out your window and ask your child to draw a picture of something you see.
2. At a park, count the number of birds that you see every ten minutes. Total the number after 30 minutes.
3. Set an alarm to go off half past the hour. Discuss what the clock looks like at this time.

Chapter 37

Today's lesson will be lots of fun as we join Bogart and Paige on an island!

While they explore, you will have a good time learning:
- Nouns
- Completing sentences
- Time by the half hour
- Greater than/less than
- Fractions

Naming Words

Draw a line from each picture to the box where it belongs.

garden

doctor

girl

school

desert

boy

People

Places

Sentences

Imagine that you are traveling into space. Draw a picture of your spaceship. Then complete the sentences below.

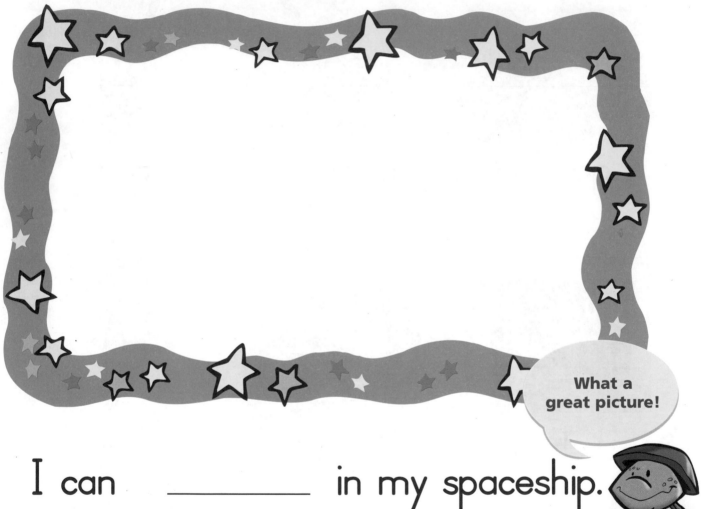

What a great picture!

I can _____ in my spaceship.

My spaceship is _____ .

It can _____ .

Drawing Clocks to the Half Hour

Draw hands on each ladybug clock to show the time.

5:30

2:30

11:30

7:30

3:30

Clocks come in all shapes and sizes!

Which One Has Less Area?

For each group, circle the one that has **less** area.

If an object takes up less space than another, it has less area.

Counting Parts of a Whole

How many parts does each picture have? Draw a line from each picture to the number of parts it has.

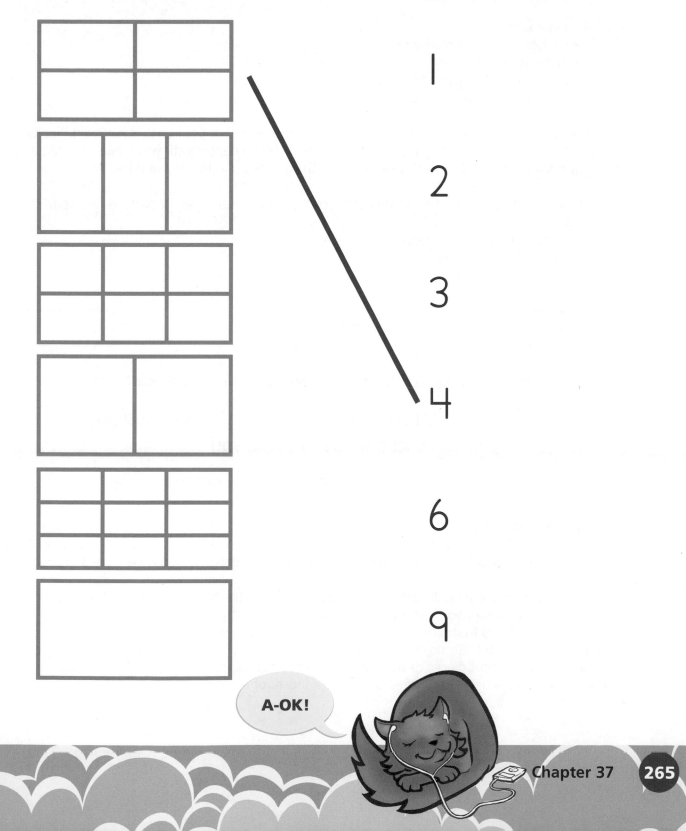

1

2

3

4

6

9

A-OK!

Assessment

Chapter 37 Review

In Chapter 37, your child studied descriptive words, telling time, and understanding parts of a whole.

Your child learned:
- Recognition of naming words.
- Sentence composition.
- Reading clocks; telling time.
- Recognition of relative size.

Do the following activities to review what your child has learned. If your child is having difficulty in any of the areas below, go back through the pages of this chapter with your child. You can also review and reinforce the skills in this section with the additional activities listed below.

1. Have your child use a pencil to divide each rectangle into the number of parts as directed.

Divide rectangle 1 into two parts.
Divide rectangle 2 into three parts.
Divide rectangle 3 into four parts.

1 [ ]   2 [ ]   3 [ ]

2. Ask your child to think about a school bus and then complete the sentences below.

Children can _____ in a school bus.
A school bus can take you _____.

Can your child think of more than one word for each of these blanks?

Additional Activities
Here are some simple and fun activities you can do with your child to practice what you have worked on in this chapter. These activities will reinforce the skills your child studied on the previous pages.

1. Help your child make a clock using a paper plate, marking the hour numbers with a pencil or pen. Ask your child to use two pencils as clock hands to demonstrate the correct time.
2. Gather several items from your kitchen. Discuss which item has the largest area. Which has the least? Group the items in pairs and decide which item in each pair has less area.
3. Using several different pieces of the same size paper, cut each piece into a different number of parts. You can discuss what makes up half or a fourth of each piece.

Chapter 38

Marco and Bogart love to watch movies! They want you to help them decide what to watch. Together, you will learn about predictions and numbers.

You will learn about:
• Making predictions
• Fractions

Now let's see what is showing at the movies!

Making Predictions

Read the story. Then circle the picture at the bottom of the page that shows what you think will happen next.

Remember to use the clues in the pictures.

Quincy loves popcorn.

He cannot wait to eat it during the movie.

The movie is about to start!

Making Predictions

Read the story below. Use the information in the pictures and the sentences to guess what will happen next. Draw a picture of the next event in this story.

I'm so sorry, Quincy! I was in such a rush to get to the movie, I didn't even see you there!

Now I have no popcorn! I sure am sad.

What do you think the man will do to cheer Quincy up?

269

Making Predictions

Read the story below. Circle the picture that shows what you think will happen next.

The boy lost his dog.

He looked all over the park.

Then he heard barking in the woods.

Great job!

Matching Parts of a Whole to Fractions

A fraction is a number that names part of a group. For example, 1/4 means 1 of 4.

Circle the baseball bat that shows the fraction of the ball that is shaded.

Coloring Parts of a Group

Color $\frac{1}{4}$ of the tops yellow.

Color $\frac{1}{3}$ of the kites blue.

Color $\frac{1}{2}$ of the blocks orange.

You color very well!

Assessment

Chapter 38 Review

In this chapter, your child studied the progression of events and basic fractions.

Your child learned:
- Recognition of sequential events.
- Anticipation of outcomes through predictive reasoning.
- Recognition of fractions.

Work with your child on the chapter review activities shown below. If your child has difficulty with any of these exercises, go back through the chapter with him or her to review the material. You can also review and reinforce these skills with your child using the exercises in the additional activities section below.

1. Have your child read the following sentences and draw a picture to show what happens next: Joe plants some flower seeds in his garden. Joe waters the seeds in his garden. The sun shines on Joe's garden.

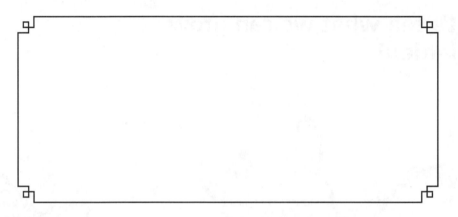

2. Direct your child to draw the lines in each box to show the fraction that is written:

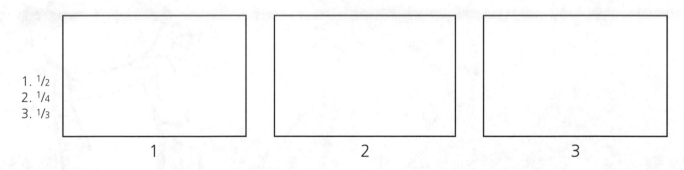

1. $\frac{1}{2}$
2. $\frac{1}{4}$
3. $\frac{1}{3}$

     1   2   3

Additional Activities

Below are some interactive ways you and your child can practice what you have worked on in this chapter. These activities will reinforce the skills your child studied on the previous pages.

1. While eating a snack, ask your child to eat a fraction of it.
2. In a sandbox at the park, draw different shapes. Ask your child to draw a line in each shape to show a fraction.
3. During the day, ask your child to predict what will happen next as you perform different routines.

Chapter 39

Paige and Rosa are playing in the garden! They want you to look at the pretty sunflowers they are growing.

You will learn about:
• Characters and setting of a story
• Main ideas
• Fractions

Now let's see what we can grow in the garden!

Characters and Setting

Read the following story. Then circle the characters from the story and write the setting.

a boy   Quincy   Zookeeper   Marco

Where did this story take place?_____

_____

Characters

Draw a picture of your favorite storybook character in the box below. Then write about your picture.

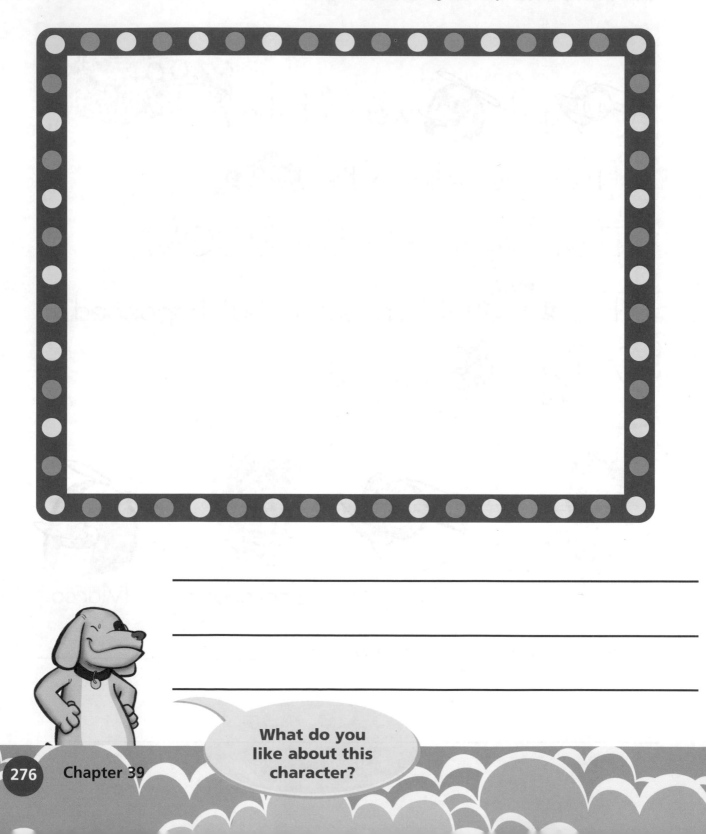

_____

_____

_____

What do you like about this character?

Key Events

Ask a grown-up to help you read the story.

The Birthday Mystery

Paige was skipping to Sally Snail's birthday party. On the way, she saw Sam. Sam looked sad. "What's the matter, Sam? Aren't you excited to go to Sally's party?"

Sam said, "I wasn't invited." Paige said, "I'm sure you were! Maybe your invitation got lost." The two friends looked everywhere for Sam's invitation. Finally, they checked in Sam's mailbox. The invitation was stuck to the back of the box! Sam was so happy!

"But I don't have a present for Sally!" Sam said. "Don't worry. Sally won't mind," said Paige. "Let's go!" At the party, Sally welcomed her friends. She said, "My best birthday present is having all my friends with me!"

Now draw pictures of three key events that happened in "The Birthday Mystery" story on the last page.

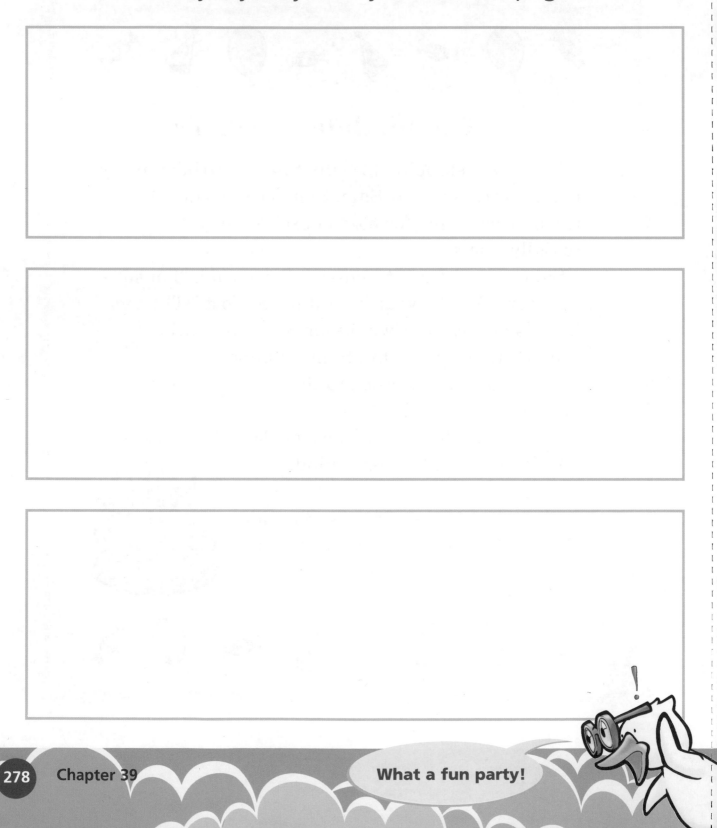

What a fun party!

Coloring Parts of a Whole for Fractions

Color the part of the pool that shows the fraction written below it.

1/2   **2/3**   **3/4**

It's so much fun being outside!

Assessment

Chapter 39 Review

In this chapter, your child studied the basic elements of storytelling and the use of fractions in objects and groups.

Your child learned:
- Recognition of characters, settings, and events.
- Recognition of parts of a group and parts of a whole.

Work with your child on the chapter review activities shown below. If your child has difficulty with any of these exercises, go back through the chapter with him or her to review the material. You can also review and reinforce these skills with your child using the exercises in the additional activities section below.

1. From page 275, ask your child to write the names of the characters in the story.

   _____   _____   _____   _____

2. From the story on page 275, ask your child to tell you the setting when Quincy, the zookeeper, and Marco were all together?

Additional Activities

Here are some simple and fun activities you can do with your child to practice what you have worked on in Chapter 39. These activities will reinforce the skills your child learned on the previous pages.

1. While reading a favorite story, ask your child about the characters and setting.
2. On the way home from the store, ask your child about some of the events that happened at the store. What happened first? What happened next? Last?
3. Collect twenty coins. Discuss what fraction are pennies, nickels, dimes, and quarters.

Chapter 40

Today's lesson will be lots of fun as we join Rosa and Sam at the movies!

While they decide which movie to see, you will learn about:
- Main ideas of a story
- Patterns using shapes
- Pattern extensions

Now let's see what fun we can have at the movies!

Key Events

Read the story. Ask a grown-up for help if you need it.

Last but Not Least!

Paige and Sam are at a parade. They cheer for their friends as they march by. They see Tim the Turtle, Betty the Blue Jay, and many of the children from school. "What fun! I wish we could be in the parade too!" said Paige. "Maybe next year," said Sam. "Now the parade is finished."

"No, it isn't!" shouted Sally the Snail. "I'm a little bit slower than all the others, so I'm the last one in the parade. Would you like to join me?" "Yes!" said Paige and Sam. They joined Sally, and they had a great time marching with their friend!

Circle the sentences below that are key events in the story.

Paige and Sam
went to the movies.

Paige and Sam
went to a parade.

Paige and Sam
marched with Sally.

After the parade,
Paige and Sam
ate dinner.

Key Events

Ask a grown-up to help you read the story.

How Grandmother Spider Stole the Sun

When Earth was new, there was no light. The animals and people lived in the dark. It was hard to live with no light. "I heard that there is something called the Sun," said Eagle. "It is on the other side of the world. Maybe we can take a piece of it!"

Fox decided that he would try to take a piece of the Sun. But when he got close to the Sun, it was so hot that his fur turned bright red. Then Possum tried to take a piece of the Sun. She had a bushy tail. She tried to take a piece of the Sun with her tail. But the Sun burned the hair off her tail! She dropped it. Next, Grandmother Spider tried. She wove a bag out of her webbing. She put a piece of the Sun in her bag and brought it back. She put the piece of Sun in the sky. Now there was light on Earth!

Cross out the pictures that do not show key events of the story.

The animals on Earth wanted light.

Grandmother Spider brought the Sun to Earth.

Eagle put the Sun in the sky.

The animals went swimming.

Some animals tried to take the Sun.

The moon was bright.

Great job!

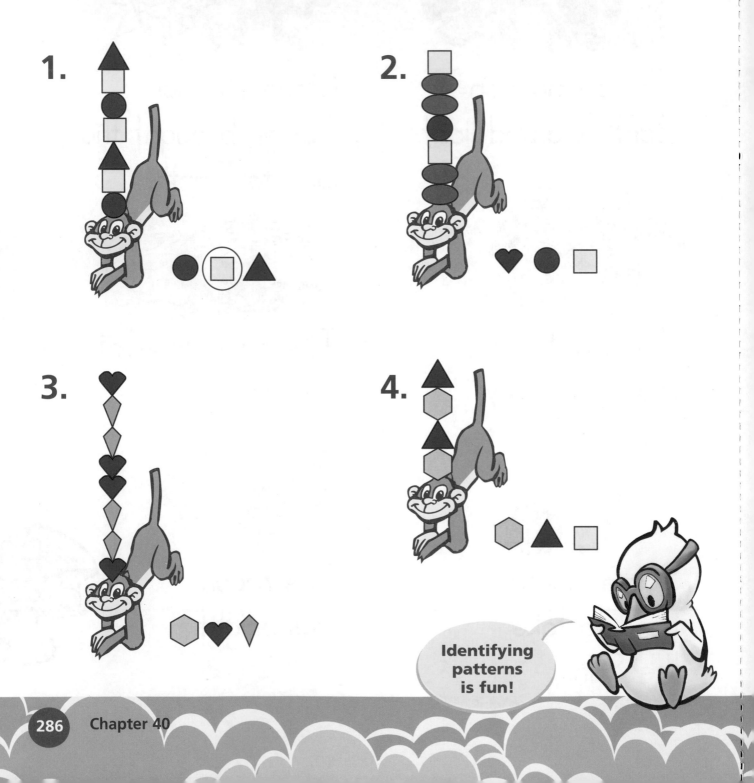

Extending Patterns of Shapes

Find the pattern in each set. Then circle the shape that would come next if stacked on top.

1.

2.

3.

4.

Identifying patterns is fun!

Assessment

Chapter 40 Review

In this chapter, your child studied key events within a story and the determining sequences of objects and numbers.

Your child learned:
- Recognition of key events.
- Identification of repeating patterns.

The following activities will provide a review of what your child has learned. If he or she has any difficulty in any of the areas below, go back through the pages of this chapter with your child. You can also review and reinforce the skills in this section with the additional activities listed below.

1. Ask your child to answer the question using the story on page 282:
   What was the first key event in the story?

2. Draw the shapes in the blanks that complete the pattern.

Additional Activities

Here are some interactive ways you and your child can practice what you have worked on in this chapter. These activities will reinforce the skills your child studied on the previous pages.

1. Read a story and discuss with your child three events that happened.
2. Ask your child to tell you his or her favorite story, and then draw a picture of a key event from that story.
3. Use items around your home for you and your child to create patterns that repeat.

Chapter 41

It's time to work in the garden, but Rosa just wants to dance! Can you and Paige get her to help out?

You will learn about:
- Story beginnings, middles, and ends
- Patterns using shapes
- Patterns using numbers

Beginning, Middle, and End

Read the story below. Draw a circle around the beginning. Put a star next to the middle. Underline the end.

Quincy wants to see a movie.

He calls his friend Marco.

They go to the movies together.

Read the directions carefully.

Beginning, Middle, and End

Look at the pictures below. They tell a story. Write what is happening in each picture to show the beginning, middle, and end of the story.

Describing Patterns of Shapes

A silly monkey has just learned how to juggle. Find the pattern and describe it using combinations of the letters A, B, and C. **Hint: Not all the patterns use all three letters.**

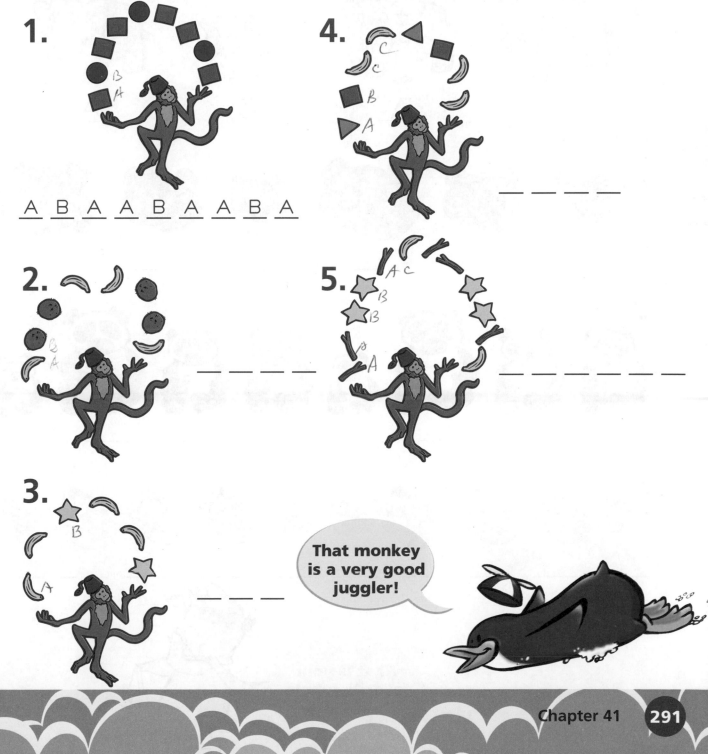

1. A B A A B A A B A

2. _ _ _ _

3. _ _ _

4. _ _ _ _

5. _ _ _ _ _

That monkey is a very good juggler!

Describing Patterns of Size

The animal families are walking through the jungle. Look for the patterns of size. Describe the patterns by using letters A, B, and C.

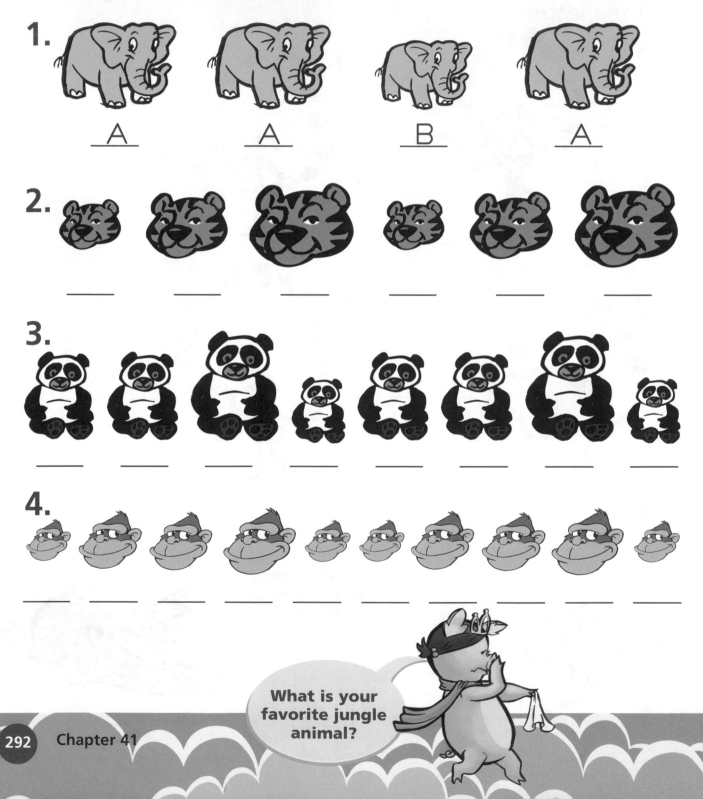

1. A   A   B   A

2. ___ ___ ___ ___ ___ ___

3. ___ ___ ___ ___ ___ ___ ___ ___

4. ___ ___ ___ ___ ___ ___ ___ ___ ___ ___

What is your favorite jungle animal?

Describing Patterns of Numbers

Decide what number is added to get the next one in the pattern. Describe the pattern you see by filling in the missing numbers.

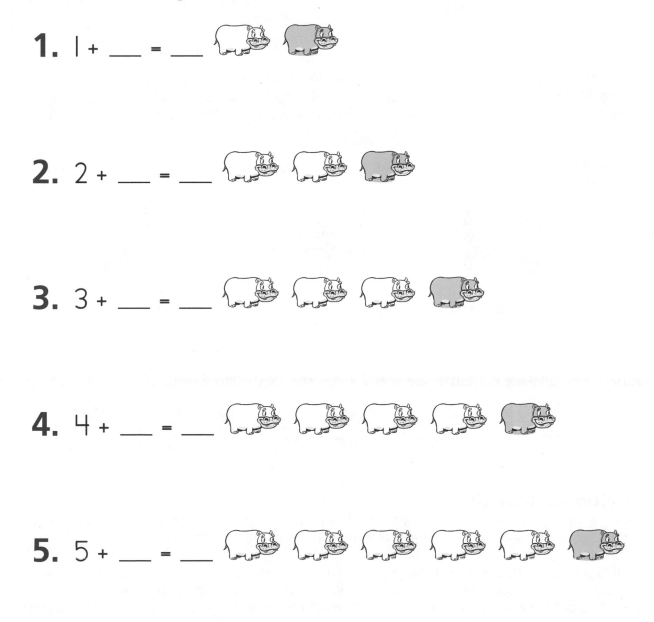

1. I + ___ = ___

2. 2 + ___ = ___

3. 3 + ___ = ___

4. 4 + ___ = ___

5. 5 + ___ = ___

Assessment

Chapter 41 Review

In this chapter, your child studied the key parts of a story and several methods for identifying sequences of objects and numbers.

Your child learned:
- Recognition of fundamental story components.
- Identification of repeating patterns.
- Description of patterns of size and shape.
- Description of numeric patterns.

Do the following activities with your child to review what your child has learned. If your child is having difficulty in any of the areas below, go back through the pages of this chapter with your child. With the additional activities listed below, you can also review and reinforce the skills covered in this chapter.

1. These pictures tell a story. Tell your child to write the numbers 1, 2, and 3 to show the order that the events occurred.

_____   _____   _____

2. Ask your child to look again at the story on the first page of this chapter, and write what happens in each picture to show the beginning, the middle, and the end.

3. Have your child use the letters A, B, and C to describe the pattern shown.

Additional Activities
Here are some simple and fun things you can do with your child to practice what you have worked on in this chapter. To help reinforce what was learned in this chapter, try these activities.

1. Help your child choose an everyday event, like getting ready for bed. Ask him or her to draw a picture of what happens first, what happens in the middle, and what happens at the end.
2. Make a pattern using your child's toys. Have your child write the letters that describe the pattern on pieces of paper and then place the correct letters next to the toy.
3. Using members of your family, have your child use letters to describe patterns of size (such as tall, short, medium).

Chapter 42

Marco loves to explore! This time he and Rosa are going to investigate the forest, and you are invited to come along!

You will learn about:
- Story beginnings, middles, and ends
- Patterns

Creating Patterns of Sounds

Look at the animals and make their sounds.

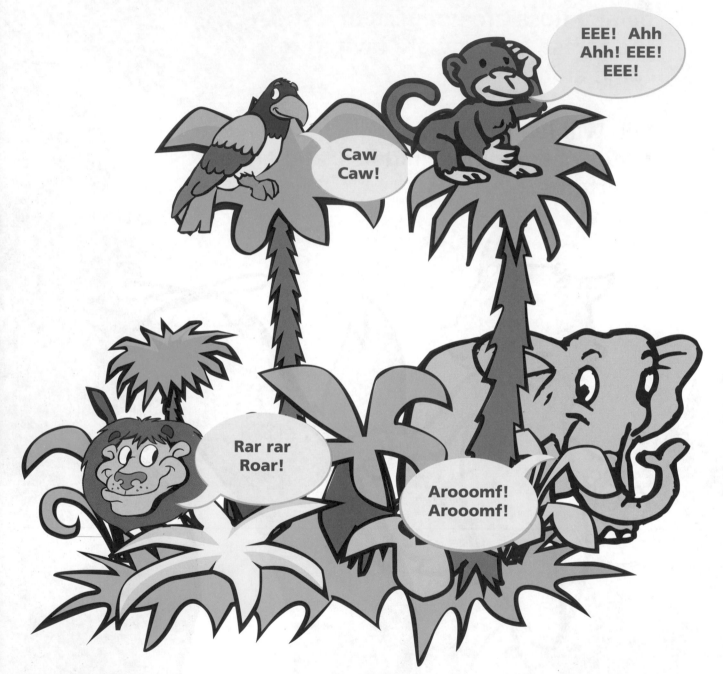

Create your own pattern using these animal sounds.
Share your pattern with a friend!

Beginning, Middle, and End

Ask a grown-up to help you read the story below.

The Fox and the Crow

One day, Crow found a large piece of cheese. She took it and flew to a high branch on a tree in the woods. Fox walked by and saw Crow in the tree. He wanted to eat the cheese. "Hello, Crow. May I have some of your cheese?" asked Fox. Crow shook her head. She did not want to share it. "Well, would you mind singing me a song? You have such a lovely voice!" Crow was amazed. No one had ever liked her singing before. She took a deep breath and started to sing, "Caw! Caw!" The cheese fell out of her mouth. It fell all the way to the ground, and Fox ate it up!

Beginning, Middle, and End

Think of a story that you know. Write the beginning, middle, and end on the lines below. Then draw a picture of the story on the next page.

Beginning

_____

_____

_____

Middle

_____

_____

_____

_____

End

_____

_____

That looks like
a great story!

Chapter 42

Beginning, Middle, and End

Look at these pictures of the fox and the crow. Put them in order by drawing a line to match the pictures to the words.

> **Reread the story if you need help remembering.**

Beginning

Middle

End

Assessment

Chapter 42 Review

Your child studied the key parts of a story and several methods for identifying sequences of objects and numbers in this chapter.

Your child learned:
- Recognition of fundamental story components.
- Storytelling.

Work with your child on the chapter review activities shown below. If your child has difficulty with any of these exercises, go back through the chapter with him or her to review the material. You can also review and reinforce these skills with your child using the exercises in the additional activities section below.

1. Have your child write a sentence to describe what happens at the beginning of the story.

2. Look again at the pictures from the first activity. Have your child draw a circle around the picture that shows the end of the story.

3. Ask your child to draw a pattern on the back of the snake using triangles and circles.

Additional Activities

Here are some simple and fun activities you can do with your child to practice what you have worked on in Chapter 42. These activities will reinforce the skills your child learned on the previous pages.

1. Help your child think of an animal you see in your neighborhood. Have your child write a story about that animal that has a beginning, middle, and end.
2. Have each member of your family choose an animal sound. Work with your family to create a pattern you can all say aloud.
3. Have your child make up a story about your family. Make sure it has a beginning, a middle, and an end.

Chapter 43

Rosa and Marco love to help out on the farm! Ride along as they learn how to drive a tractor.

You will learn about:
- Gathering information from the text
- Characters
- Making predictions
- Understanding directions
- Graphing

Gathering Information

Look at the picture. Read what Paige says about the elephant. Then write the answers to the questions below.

> An elephant has a trunk. It can use it to pick up leaves.

What does an elephant have?

_____

What is the elephant doing with its trunk?

_____

> I wonder what else elephants can do?

Characters

Draw a line to match the names to the characters.

The Three Bears

Gingerbread Man

The Frog Prince

Princess

Do you know any stories with these characters?

Making Predictions

Read the story and look at the picture.
Then write the next part of this story.

Look at the picture carefully!

The movie will start soon! Quincy will
be late if he walks to the theater. He
doesn't want to miss the movie, so he

_____

_____

_____

Understanding Directions

Play this game with a friend.

With a sheet of paper and pencil, sit with your back against your friend's back.

Draw three shapes on your sheet of paper. Now describe them to your friend and see if your friend can name them.

Then have your friend draw three shapes and describe them to you.

It's lots of fun!

Use words to help describe these shapes, such as:

- above
- below
- right
- left
- next to
- under
- touching
- upside down

Using Ordered Pairs

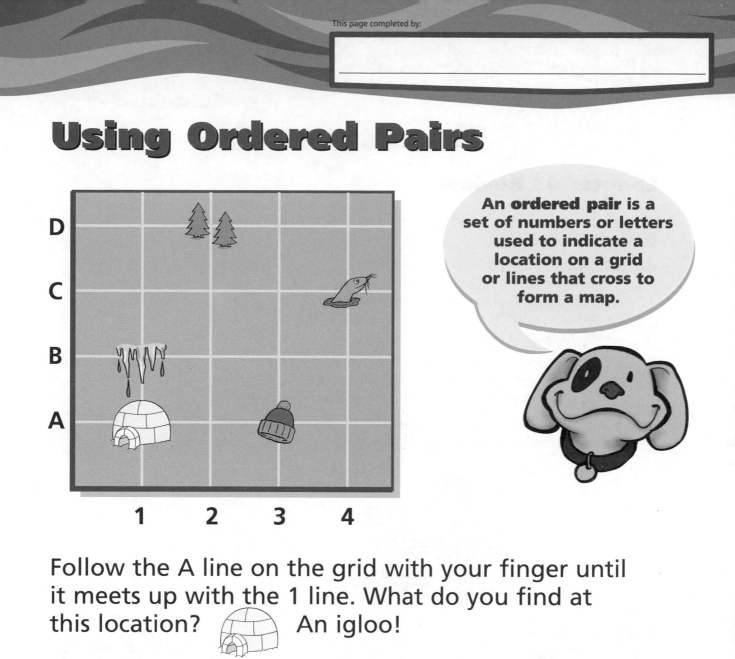

An **ordered pair** is a set of numbers or letters used to indicate a location on a grid or lines that cross to form a map.

Follow the A line on the grid with your finger until it meets up with the 1 line. What do you find at this location? An igloo!

Circle the object that is found at B1

Circle the object that is found at A3

Circle the object that is found at D2

Circle the object that is found at C4

Assessment

Chapter 43 Review

In this chapter, your child studied gathering information, making predictions, describing objects, and locating objects on a grid.

Your child learned:
- Identification of information within a story.
- Prediction of events based on visual information.
- Verbal description of objects.
- Use of ordered pairs.

To review what your child has learned, do the two activities below. If your child is having difficulty in any of the areas below, go back and review the pages with him or her. You can also review and reinforce the skills in this section with the additional activities listed below.

1. Ask your child to read the sentences and then answer the following questions:
   "Tom has a shovel and he can dig a hole with it."

   What does Tom have? Tom has a _____ .
   What can Tom do with the tool he has? Tom can _____.

2. On the grid, have your child draw a circle on the grid at C1.
   Then, draw a heart on the grid at B3.
   Finally, draw a square on the grid at D4.

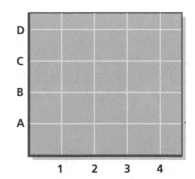

Additional Activities
Here are some interactive ways you and your child can practice what you have worked on in this chapter. These activities will reinforce the skills your child studied on the previous pages.

1. Draw a simple grid (similar to the one on page 307 of this chapter) on a large piece of paper. Ask your child to place toys on specific locations.
2. Name characters from favorite stories and ask your child to draw a picture of each character.
3. Gather a few family photographs. Ask your child questions about each photograph. Ask questions that allow your child to gather information about the event beyond "Who is in the photograph?"

Chapter 44

Bogart fell on his back while exploring the desert. He needs you and Quincy to think of a way to get him back on his feet again.

You will learn about:
- Comprehension
- Gathering information from the text
- Using a number line

Now let's see what we can find in the desert!

Answering Questions

Look at these animals! Then read the sentences.
Write answers to the questions.

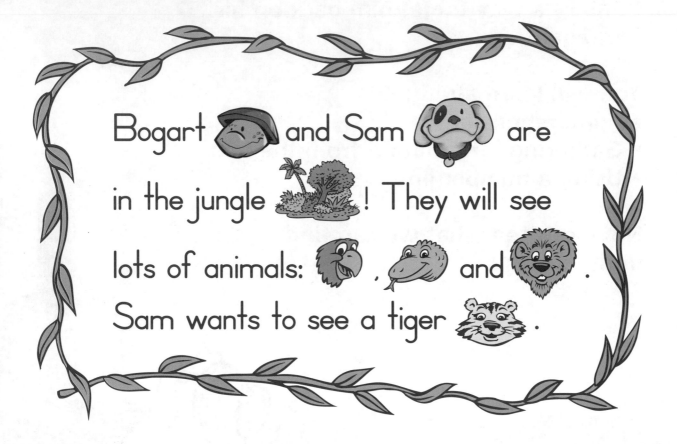

Where are Bogart and Sam? _____

What will they see? _____

What does Sam want to see? _____

Animals
are amazing!

Answering Questions

What animal is this? Connect the dots to find out. Then read the sentences and answer the questions.

Bogart sees this animal.

It is big and gray.

It lives in the jungle.

What is this animal? _____

What color is it? _____

Where does it live? _____

Gathering Information

What else can an elephant do with its trunk?
Read the sentences and look at the pictures.
Then answer the question.

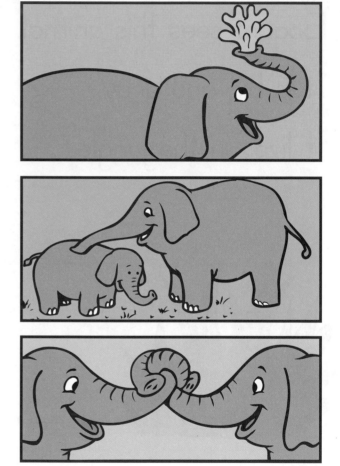

It can spray water on itself.

It can pat a baby.

Elephants can hug!

What are three things an elephant can do with its trunk? _____

_____

_____

Using a Number Line

Remember, numbers on a number line are arranged in order from left to right.

Draw the object that is 3 to the **right** of the snowman.

Draw the object that is 3 to the **left** of the penguin.

Identifying Slides

Circle the movement that is a **slide**.

A **slide** is the movement of an object from one position to another without changing the way it looks.

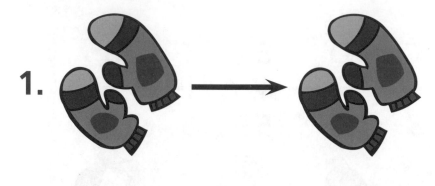

1.

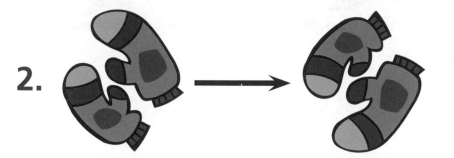

2.

3.

Geometry is the study of shapes.

Assessment

Chapter 44 Review

In this chapter, your child studied how to gather information and answer questions, how to use a number line and identifying slides.

Your child learned:
- Comprehension, analysis, and discernment of information.
- Use of a number line.
- Recognition of objects relocated with a slide motion.

To review what your child has learned, do the 3 activities below. If your child is having difficulty in any of the areas below, go back and review the pages with him or her. You can also review and reinforce the skills in this section with the additional activities listed below.

1. Johnny and Kat are in the grocery store. They see lots of fruits and vegetables. Johnny wants to buy oranges. Kat wants to buy the grapes.

Have your child read the sentences and write the answer to these questions.

Where are Johnny and Kat? _____

What did Johnny want to buy? _____

2. Using the story in the first activity, ask your child to complete the sentences below.

At the store Johnny and Kat see _____.

Kat wants to buy _____.

3. Instruct your child to draw the object that is 2 to the right of the sled.
   Next, have your child draw the object that is 3 to the left of the object you just drew.

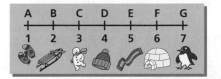

Additional Activities
Below are some interactive ways you and your child can review what you have worked on in this chapter. These activities will reinforce the skills your child studied on the previous pages.

1. While at the zoo, give clues about certain animals. After your child guesses the animal ask some questions about that animal.
2. Using chalk on the sidewalk, draw a number line. Give your child directions as he/she moves up and down the number line.
3. Find a pair of objects in your home. (such as shoes, gloves an the like) Have your child use them to demonstrate a movement that is a slide and that isn't a slide.

Chapter 45

Rosa and Quincy are having an airplane adventure! They want you to ride along with them and help them stay on course.

You will learn about:
• Comprehension
• Gathering information from the text
• Understanding directions

Now let's see what we can find in the clouds!

Answering Questions

Read the sentences. Then answer the questions.

Sam went to a store.

He bought a toy monkey!

He put it in a box.

He gave it to Paige!

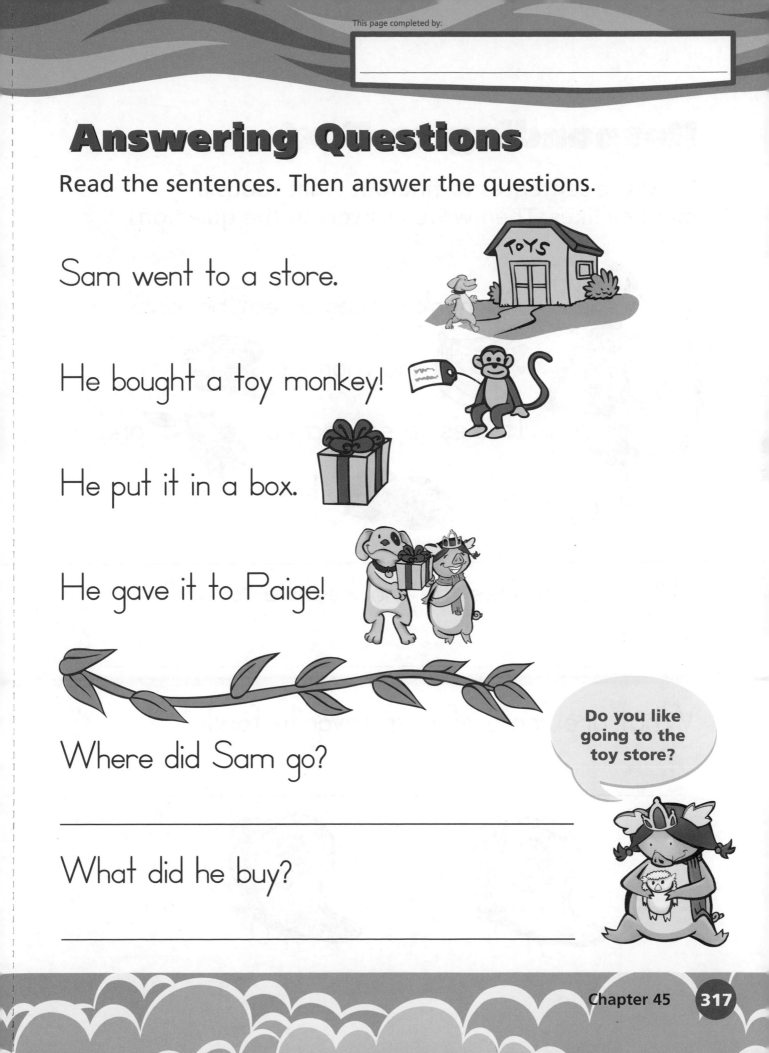

Where did Sam go?

Do you like going to the toy store?

_____

What did he buy?

_____

Responding to Text

Read the sentences to find out what foods a monkey likes. Then write answers to the questions.

A monkey likes to eat bananas and mangos. It likes to eat leaves and nuts, too.

What foods does the monkey like to eat?

_____

What are some of your favorite foods?

_____

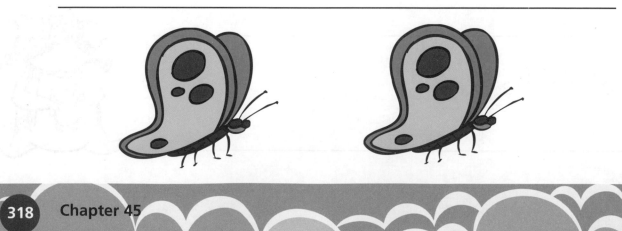

Responding to Text

My grandpa helps me bake cookies!

Read the story below. Then write answers to the questions.

1. Can I eat the leaf?

2. I cannot get it!

3. Now can you get it?

4. Thanks, Mom!

How did the mother monkey help the baby?

_____

How does a grown-up in your home help you?

_____

Drawing Slides

Draw some slides.

> Remember, a **slide** is the movement of an object from one position to another without changing the way it looks.

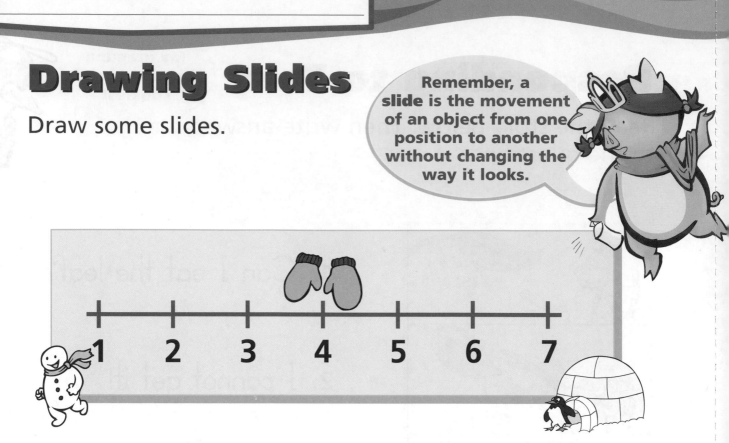

Draw another pair of mittens 2 places to the right.

Draw another pair of mittens 3 places to the left.

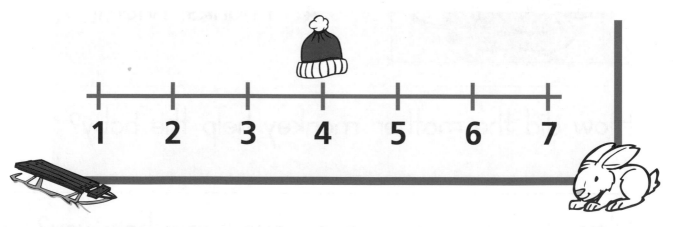

Draw another hat 1 place to the left.

Draw another hat 3 places to the right.

Drawing Flips

Trace and color the flips.

Remember, a **flip** is the movement of an object from one position to another by flipping it over a line.

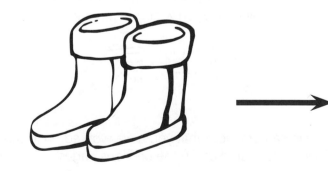 

Assessment

Chapter 45 Review

In this chapter, your child studied answering questions, responding to text, and identifying slides and flips.

Your child learned:
- Comprehension of written information.
- Use of a number line.
- Recognition of objects relocated with a slide motion.
- Recognition of objects relocated with a flip motion.

To review what your child has learned, do the activities below. Review the pages of this chapter with your child if he or she is having difficulty in any of the areas below. You can also review and reinforce the skills in this section with the additional activities listed below.

1. Have your child read the sentences and then answer the questions:
   "In the winter, Erin likes to play outside in the snow. She likes to sled and throw snowballs. She likes to build a snowman, too."

   What does Erin like to do in the snow? _____

   What do you like to do in the snow? _____

2. Have your child study the number line shown and draw another snowman 4 places to the right.

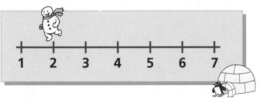

3. Ask your child to circle the pictures that show a slide and draw an X on the pictures that show a flip.

Additional Activities
Here are some interactive ways you and your child can practice what you have worked on in this chapter. These activities will reinforce the skills your child studied on the previous pages.

1. Ask your child about some of the things his/her favorite story character likes. Then ask your child what things he/she likes that are the same or different from that character.
2. Use a ruler for a number line. Have your child demonstrate slides with a few toys.
3. Ask your child and family members to demonstrate a slide and a flip with their body on the floor.

Chapter 46

Quincy loves to explain things. While the teacher is away, he tries to take over the classroom. Not everyone listens to him, though.

You will learn about:
- Gathering information from the text
- Understanding directions

Now let's have some fun in the classroom!

Answering Questions

Look at the picture and read the sentences.
Then answer the questions with **yes** or **no**.

Snakes have scales.

They do not have any legs.

They have long tongues.

Do snakes have scales? _____

Do snakes have legs? _____

Gathering Information

Have a grown-up help you read the story below.
Then answer the questions.

Once upon a time, a monkey met a leopard. "I like your spots," the monkey said. "I wish I looked like you." So the monkey found some paint and gave himself some spots. The leopard said, "You do not look like a leopard to me." The monkey looked at himself in a mirror and said, "I agree. I look very silly!" So he washed the spots off. From then on, he was happy to be a monkey!

What did the monkey want? _____

How did he get his wish? _____

_____

Answering Questions

Read what Sam wrote about the hippo.
Then write answers to the questions.

A hippo has a home in the water.
The hippo has webbed toes that
help it swim.

Where is the hippo's home? _____

What kind of toes does a hippo have?

_____

How do the toes help the hippo?

_____

Drawing Turns

Trace and color the turns.

Remember, a **turn** is the movement of an object from one position to another by turning it around a point.

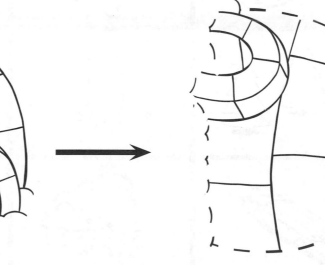

Understanding Directions

When a person is facing North, the direction that is to his or her **left** is the **west**.

North

West ← Left

East

South

Color the object to the **left** of each snowman.

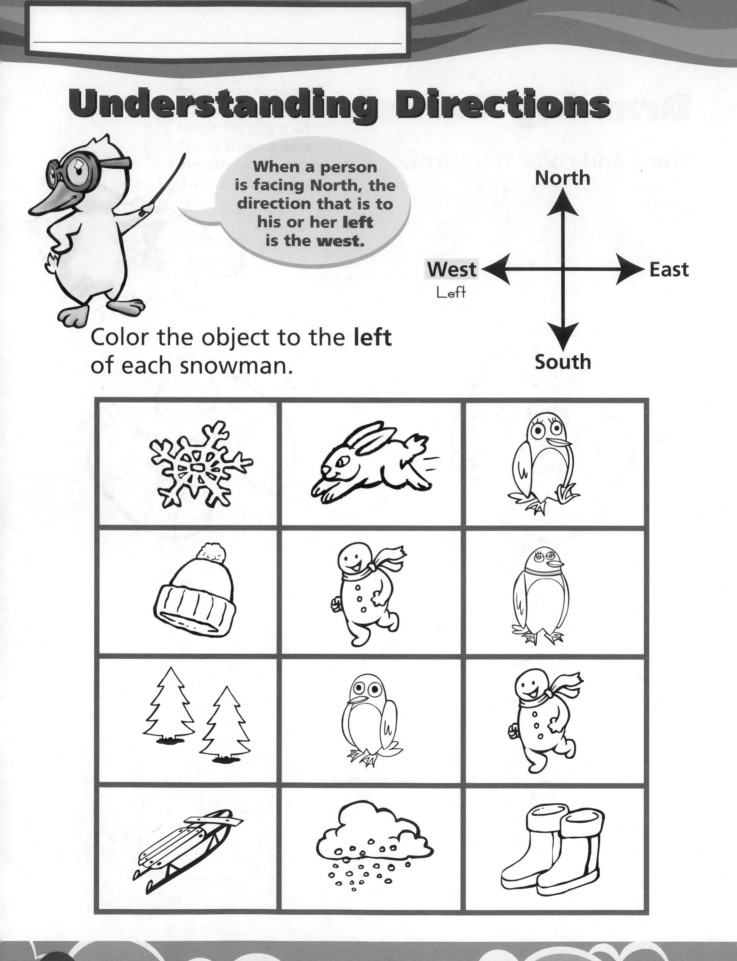

Assessment

Chapter 46 Review

In this chapter, your child studied gathering information and answering questions, identifying turns, and understanding directions.

Your child learned:
- Comprehension of written information.
- Recognition of objects relocated with a turning motion.
- Recognition of directional information.

Do the following activities to review what your child has learned. If your child is having difficulty in any of the areas below, go back through the pages of this chapter with your child. With the additional activities listed below, you can also review and reinforce the skills covered in this chapter.

1. "Dogs have fur. They do not have hooves. They have four paws."
   Have your child answer each question with yes or no.

   Do dogs have fur? _____
   Do dogs have hooves? _____
   Do dogs have four paws? _____

2. Have your child look at the heart. Next to the arrow, tell the child to draw the heart to show a turn.

3. Have your child look at the pictures and answer the questions:

   What object is to the left of the boots? _____
   What object is to the left of the rabbit? _____

Additional Activities

Below are some interactive ways you and your child can review what you have worked on in this chapter. These activities will reinforce the skills your child studied on the previous pages.

1. From your child's toys, choose a stuffed animal. Talk about the animal with your child. Then ask questions about the toy that your child can answer "yes" or "no."
2. After reading a story, have your child ask you a few questions about what happened in the story.
3. Take a walk with your child, taking only left turns. Point out when you turn left and when you are traveling west.

Chapter 47

Marco and Quincy are exploring a cave! You can come along with them to see an amazing underground world.

As you do, you will learn about:
• Gathering information from text
• Understanding directions

Now let's see what we can find underground!

Gathering Information

Look at the picture and ask a grown-up to help you read the information. Then complete the sentences under the picture.

Parrots are a kind of bird. Some parrots are very colorful. Parrots eat seeds and fruits. Some of them eat bugs, too. Many parrots can copy sounds they hear.

Parrots are a kind of _____ .

Some parrots are very _____ .

Parrots eat things like _____

Answering Questions

Read the Tiger Facts. Then answer the questions under the pictures.

Tiger Facts

A tiger is a big cat. A baby tiger is called a cub. Tigers have stripes. Tigers have sharp claws. Tigers have sharp teeth. Tigers can swim and climb trees.

What is a tiger? _____

What is a baby tiger called? _____

What can tigers do? _____

Answering Questions

Sam and Marco are visiting a rain forest. Look at the picture and read the sentences. Then answer the questions.

This is a red-eyed frog.
It likes a wet home.
Red-eyed frogs sleep in the day.
They hunt for food at night.

How did the frog get its name?_____

_____

Where does it like to live?_____

When do the frogs sleep?_____

_____

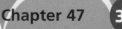

I love all kinds of frogs!

Chapter 47   333

Figuring Things Out

To get to the igloo, Sam walked four blocks down, two blocks left, one block up, three blocks right, and two blocks down. On which color did he start?

HINT: Work backward!

Step 1: Start at the igloo, and go 2 blocks _____.

Step 2: Then Sam walked 3 blocks right, so go _____ blocks _____.

Step 3: Then Sam walked 1 block up, so go _____ block _____.

Step 4: Then Sam walked 2 blocks left, so go _____ blocks _____.

Step 5: Then Sam walked 4 blocks down, so go _____ blocks _____.

At what color did you wind up? _____

That was cool!

Thinking Things Through

Use these clues to decide which child made which snow angel. Write the child's name on the snow angel he or she made.

Claude and Suzanne are to the **right** and **left** of Jose.

Claude is **not** on the left of Jose.

Maria and Jimmy are **above** and **below** Jose.

Maria is **not** above Jose.

Janet is to the **left** of Maria.

Derek is **above** Claude.

Jose

Look at all the snow angels!

Assessment

Chapter 47 Review

In this chapter, your child studied how to gather information, answer questions, follow directions, and think and reason.

Your child learned:
- Comprehension of written information.
- Following instructions.
- Recognition of directional information.
- Problem solving.

The following activities will provide a review of what your child has learned. If he or she has any difficulty in any of the areas below, go back through the pages of this chapter with your child. You can also review and reinforce the skills in this section with the additional activities listed below.

1. After again reading the information on page 331, have your child answer the following question:

   What can parrots copy? _____

2. Reading the information on page 332 of this chapter, ask your child to complete the sentence below:

   Tigers have _____ and sharp _____ and sharp _____.

3. Direct your child to look back to the snow angels on page 335. Have your child use the information he or she filled in to answer this question:

   Who made the snow angels on the top row?

   _____   _____

Additional Activities
Here are some simple and fun activities you can do with your child to practice what you have worked on in Chapter 47. These activities will reinforce the skills your child learned on the previous pages.

1. Go to the library with your child. Read books that contain animal facts. Ask your child questions about what has been read.
2. Using the library books again, read animal facts and ask your child to draw a picture to show the animal you have described.
3. Gather friends and family. Group people on the sidewalk using the words right, left, above, and below.

Chapter 48

It's time to test Quincy's strength!
Everyone wants to see how
he will do. Can you help him
lift the big hammer?

By helping each other, you will learn about:
• Gathering information from text
• Characters and setting of a story
• Understanding directions

Now let's test our
mental strength!

Gathering Information

Look at the pictures and read the words below. Ask a grown-up to help you. Then answer the questions!

Life Cycle of a Frog

eggs

young tadpole

frog

growing tadpole

We learn a lot in the jungle!

First, frogs lay eggs in the water.
The eggs hatch into tadpoles.
Then, the tadpoles grow legs and arms.
Finally, they grow into frogs!

A tadpole has a nickname. It's a polliwog!

What happens to the eggs?

_____

What do the tadpoles grow?

_____

Characters and Setting

Read the story. Then answer the questions.

Who and Where?

Jen climbed until she was taller than anything around her. "I can see everything from up here!" she shouted. Meg yelled, "I'm going so fast! You have to try this new slide!" Max saw Jen and Meg. "Hey there!" he said. "I've been looking for you two! Mom sent me to get you for dinner!"

Who are the characters in this story?

Jen   Meg   and   Max

What is the setting of this story? Circle it.

a playground

Picturing Things

Follow the clues each child gives you to find out who built the snowman. Then circle the person who built the snowman.

Who built the snowman? _____

Drawing a Picture

Draw a ⛄ left of the 🪧.

Draw a 🐧 right of 🐧.

Draw an ⛺ behind the 🐧.

Draw a ❄ above the 🪧.

Excellent work!

Assessment

Chapter 48 Review

In Chapter 48, your child studied gathering information, identifying story settings and characters, problem solving, and understanding directions.

Your child learned:
- Comprehension of written information.
- Identification of essential story elements.
- Recognition of directional information.
- Visual reasoning.

Do the following activities to review what your child has learned. If your child is having difficulty in any of the areas below, go back through the pages of this chapter with your child. You can also review and reinforce the skills in this section with the additional activities listed below.

1. "Max and Jen and Meg went home for dinner. Mom put the pizza on the table and sat down to eat with them."
   Have your child read the story above and then answer the questions:

   Who are the characters in this story? _____

   What is the setting of this story? _____

2. Have your child go back to page 334 and draw the location of Marge's snowman. Ask your child to tell you who built the snowmen above and below Marge's snowman.

3. Direct your child to do the following:

   Draw a bird above the tree.
   Draw a flower below the tree.
   Draw a dog to the right of the tree.

Additional Activities

Below are some interactive ways you and your child can review what you have worked on in this chapter. These activities will reinforce the skills your child studied on the previous pages.

1. Go to the library and find a book about the lifecycles of different animals.
2. After your child watches a favorite show on television, ask who the characters were and where the story took place.
3. Use the board from a game of checkers. Give your child directions for placing items on the board. Use words such as down, left, and right.

343

Chapter 49

[tɔ:s] 扔球, 投掷, 翻腾,

Marco loves to toss the ball around on the beach, but Bogart is too tired to play. Can you catch the ball?

By joining the fun, you will learn about:
- Prediction making [pri'dik∫ən] 预言.预报
- Event sequence
- Understanding directions

Now let's bounce along to learning!

bounce   [bauns]
弹回, 弹起, 跳跃, 吹牛, 说大话,
拍, 反跳, 轰墙 吓唬,
解雇, 撵走 跳出跳区

Recognizing Patterns of Numbers

Find the number pattern and complete it.

2, 4, 6, _8_, ___, ___, ___, ___, ___, _20_

Add 2 to each number to show the pattern.

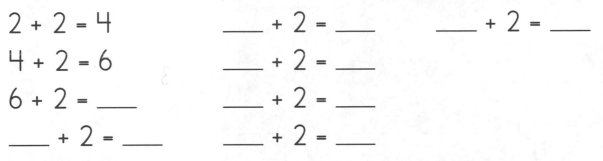

2 + 2 = 4   ___ + 2 = ___   ___ + 2 = ___

4 + 2 = 6   ___ + 2 = ___

6 + 2 = ___   ___ + 2 = ___

___ + 2 = ___   ___ + 2 = ___

Connect the dots in order to complete the pattern.

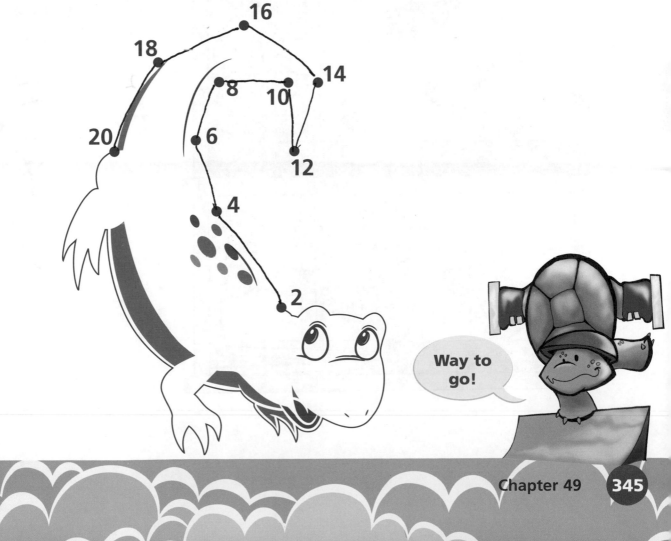

Way to go!

Putting Events in Order

Look at the pictures below. Put them in order by writing **1**, **2**, or **3** in the box for each picture.

3

Think about the order in which things happen.

2

1

Identifying Flips

Circle the movement that is a **flip**.

A **flip** is the movement of an object from one position to another by flipping it over a line.

1.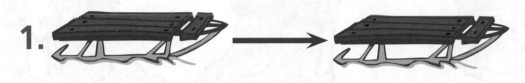

2.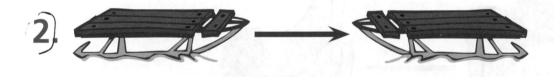

3.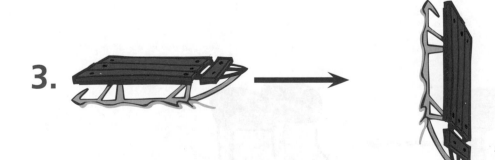

This page completed by: ______________________

Identifying Turns

A **turn** is the movement of an object from one position to another by turning it around a point.

Circle the movement that is a **turn.**

1. 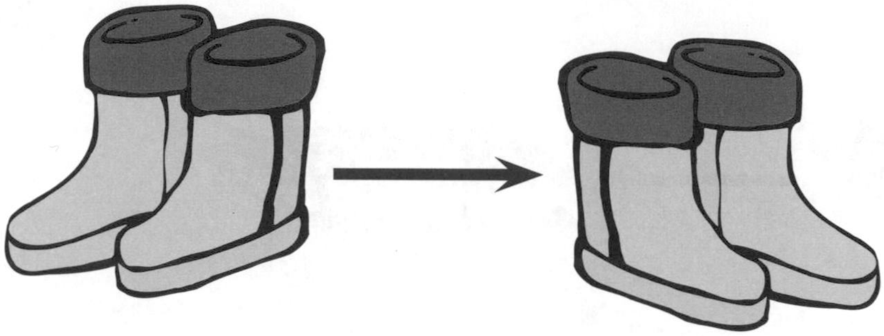

2. 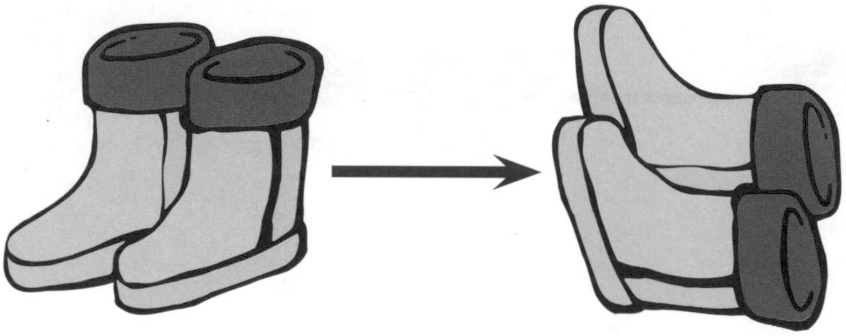

3. 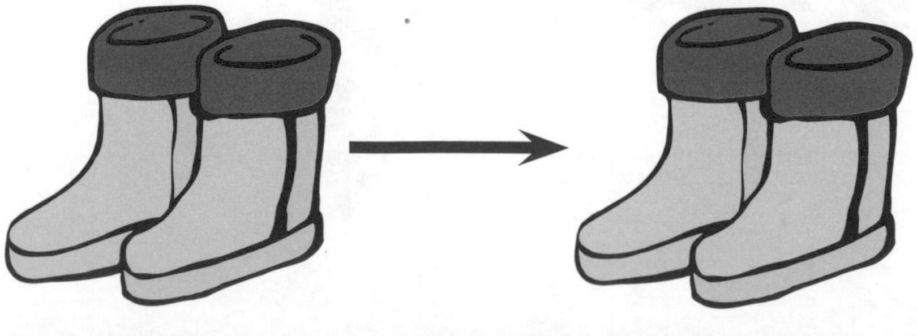

Identifying Moved Objects

Color the slides green.
Color the flips red.
Color the turns blue.

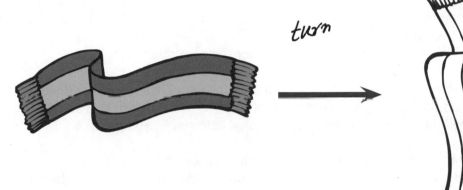

turn

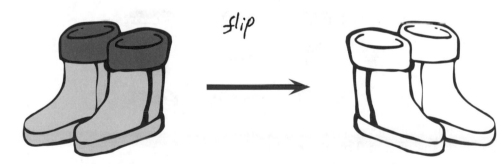

flip

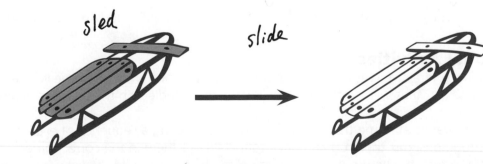

sled   slide

Assessment

Chapter 49 Review

In this chapter, your child studied how to make predictions, put events in order, and identify flips, turns, and slides.

Your child learned:
- Comprehension of written information.
- Comprehension of event sequences.
- Recognition of objects relocated with a turning, flipping, or sliding motion.

Do the following activities to review what your child has learned. If your child is having difficulty in any of the areas below, go back through the pages of this chapter with your child. You can also review and reinforce the skills in this section with the additional activities listed below.

1. "Julius went to school." "Julius brushed his teeth." "Julius woke up."
   Have your child read the sentences above and write what happened first as Julius starts his day.

   _____.

2. Direct your child to do the following:

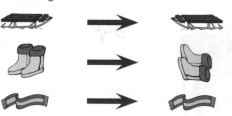

   Circle the picture that shows a flip.
   Draw and X on the picture that shows a turn.
   Underline the picture that shows a slide.

3. "Judy put on her boots. Judy put on her coat. Judy put on her hat and gloves."
   Have your child cross out the sentences that will not happen next:

   ˅   ˅
   "Judy will go to her room."   "Judy will eat dinner."   "Judy will go outside."

Additional Activities

Here are some interactive ways you and your child can practice what you have worked on in this chapter. These activities will reinforce the skills your child studied on the previous pages.

1. Take photographs at home that show your child completing a sequence of events. After developing the photographs, mix them up and have your child put them in the correct order.
2. Look at a picture in a newspaper or magazine and have your child predict what might happen next.
3. Use socks and mittens to line up a pattern of slide, flip, turn, slide, flip, turn.

Chapter 50

Everybody loves to play and splash at the beach. As you frolic along with them, you will learn about:

- Event sequence
- Story beginnings, middles, and ends
- Direction comprehension
- Numerical patterns

Now let's go have some fun in the sun!

[ˈfrɑlik] 欢乐, 嬉戏, 嬉闹, 作乐, 欢乐相聚会 (游戏)

[siːkwəns]

[ˈpætən]

[ˈnjuːmerɪkəl] 数字的, 数值, 以数字表示的

splash
溅, 泼, 溅起水花
扑通一声地

direction [dɪˈrekʃən]
方向, 方位, 范围域, 指导, 指挥, 管理
指示, 用法, 说明, 走势, 倾向

comprehension [ˌkɑmprɪˈhenʃən]
理解, 理解力, 包含, 包含力

Putting Events in Order

Now read a story about a tiger who did not want to go to bed without his bear. Show what the order of the pictures should be by writing numbers in the boxes.

Time for bed.

I can't sleep without my bear.

Now I can sleep.

Here is your bear.

[handwritten annotations: 空们，扰裂，牛店，戏弄，把戏弱斜]
[handwritten: trick 味摘，恶作剧 戏弄]
[handwritten: 欺诈，欺骗，诈骗，隐好]

Beginning, Middle, and End

Paige and Sam are watching a movie about a boy who liked to trick people. Have a grown-up help you read this story.

[handwritten: 戏弄人]

The Boy Who Cried Wolf

[handwritten: flock (flok) 羊群，人群，信众，信徒，一家子女，聚集]

There was a boy who took care of a large flock of sheep. He took them to places where they could eat grass. He made sure they stayed together. He also made sure to protect them from wolves. *[handwritten: chase (tʃeis) 追逐，追捕，追赶，赶出，驱逐，追求，争吃]*

One day, the boy was bored. He decided to play a trick on the people of the village. "Wolf! Wolf!" he shouted. The villagers ran to help the boy chase away the wolf. The boy laughed. "There is no wolf," he said. The next day, the boy played the trick again. "Wolf! Wolf!" he shouted. Once again, the villagers rushed to help him. They found no wolf. The day after that, a wolf came and started chasing the boy's sheep. "Wolf! Wolf!" he shouted. But the villagers thought the boy was playing his trick again. No one came to help.

That evening, the boy returned to the village crying. All his sheep had run away. "What happened?" asked the villagers. "There was a big wolf. It chased my sheep away! Why didn't you come help me?" the boy said. One kind woman answered, "No one believes a liar, even when he tells the truth. Don't worry. Tomorrow we will all help look for your sheep."

The pictures from the story are out of order. Put them in order by writing **1** for the beginning picture, **2** and **3** for the middle pictures, and **4** for the end picture.

You did it!

Drawing Moved Objects

Help Sam draw his winter clothes the right way.

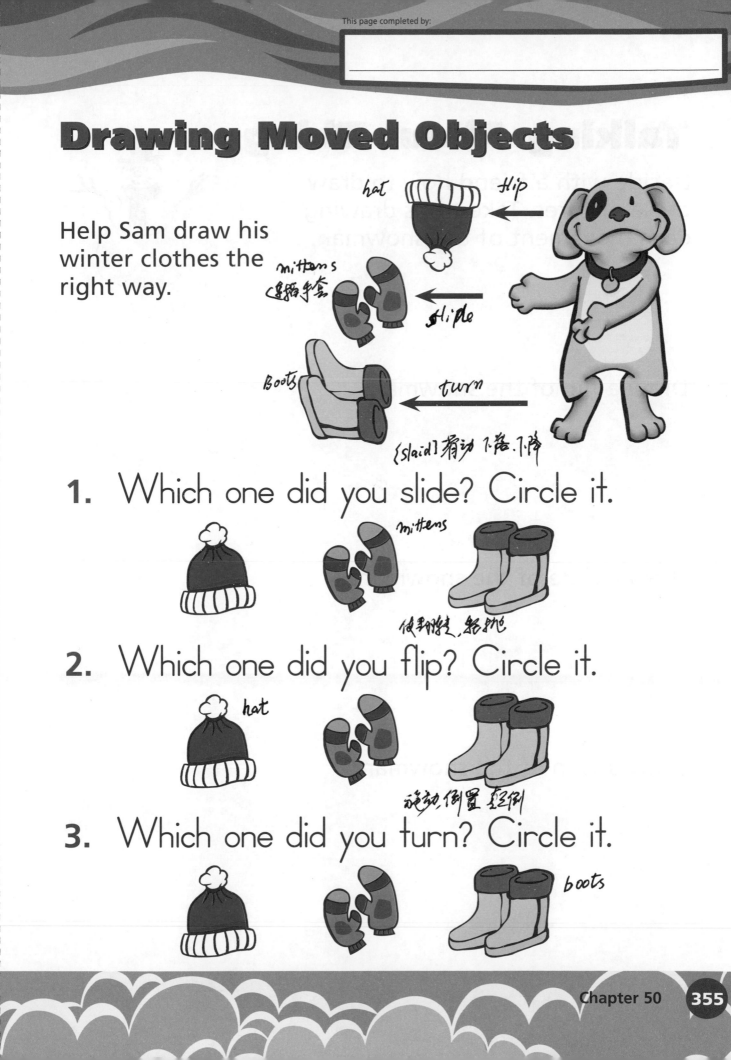

hat

flip

mittens 連指手套

slide

Boots

turn

{slaid} 滑动 下落. 下降

1. Which one did you slide? Circle it.

mittens

使翻转. 轻弹

2. Which one did you flip? Circle it.

hat

施动 倒置 翻倒

3. Which one did you turn? Circle it.

boots

Talking About Things

Decide with a friend how to draw these pictures. Take turns drawing each movement of this snowman.

Draw a flip of the snowman.

Draw a slide of the snowman.

Draw a turn of the snowman.

Assessment

recognize ['rekəgnaiz] 认定 认证 认定 识别 / 认清 辨识 确认.

Chapter 50 Review

In this chapter, your child studied putting events in order, understanding sequences of events, recognizing patterns of numbers, and identifying flips, turns, and slides.

[ai'dentifai] 确定 发现. 确认 鉴定 验明

Your child learned:

[kompri'henʃən] 理解, 包含

- Comprehension of written information.
- Comprehension of event sequences.
- Recognition of objects relocated with a turning, flipping, or sliding motion.
- Identification of numeric patterns. ['ri:ləu keit] 重新安置

Work with your child on the chapter review activities shown below. If your child has difficulty with any of these exercises, go back through the chapter with him or her to review the material. You can also review and reinforce these skills with your child using the exercises in the additional activities section below.

1. Using the story "The Boy Who Cried Wolf" in this chapter, ask your child to write what happened first.

    The boy took the sheep _____.

2. Work with your child to decide how to complete the pattern. On a separate piece of paper, draw a simple car. Then, have your child draw the car in this pattern: flip, turn, slide, flip, turn, and slide.

Additional Activities

Here are some simple and fun activities you can do with your child to practice what you have worked on in this chapter. These activities will reinforce the skills your child studied on the previous pages.

1. While doing a puzzle with your child, give directions for fitting the pieces together using the words turn and slide.
2. Make a paper doll. Cut the pieces apart. Tell your child to put it back together using the words turn, flip, and slide.
3. Have your child draw a picture of four events that take place during the day. Mix them up and have your child put them back in order.

Answer Key

Chapter 1
Answer Key

Page 7 – G, H, I, J, K, L, M, N.

Page 8 – D, E, F, G, H.

        S, T, U, V, W.

        K, L, M ,N, O.

Page 9 – a, b, c,   d, e, f,   g, h, i,   j, k, l,   m, n, o

Page 10 – Add 5 small blocks.

         Add 6 small blocks.

         Add 1 small block.

         Add 8 small blocks.

Page 11 – Color 4 sticks and 1 small block.

         Color 3 sticks and 7 small blocks.

         Color 1 stick and 4 small blocks.

         Color 5 sticks and 0 small blocks.

Page 12 – 20, 16.

         18, 17.

         20, 19.

         16, 19.

Assessment Activities—

     1. c, f, i.

     2. Color 3 sticks.

      Color 1 stick and 5 small blocks.

      Color 4 sticks and 5 small blocks.

      Color 3 sticks and 5 small blocks.

     3. 0, 1, 2, 3, 4, 5, 6, 7, 8, 9, 10, 11, 12, 13, 14, 15, 16, 17, 18, 19, 20.

Chapter 2
Answer Key

Page 15 – r, s, t, u, v, w, x, y, z.

Page 16 – In ABC order: efg, qrs, nop.

      – Not in ABC order: kba, zvy, lim.

Page 17 – (1-100)

Page 18 – 24 green blocks, 35 yellow blocks, 40 blue blocks.

Page 19 – 44.

Assessment Activities—

     1. d, g, h, l, n, p.

     2. 13, 17, 18, 20.

     3. 11, 29, 2.

Answer Key

Chapter 3
Answer Key
Page 22 – Not in ABC order: lock, water, tub; house, horn, grass; net, box, candle.

Page 23 – In ABC order: fish, gate, house; queen, robe, star; ice, jam, kite; bat, car, dust.

Page 24 – Blue = 6, 32, 12, 49, 43, 39, 24, 17; Yellow = 73, 91, 56, 85, 64.

Page 25 – 33, 55, 65; 11, 31, 50.

Page 26 – 50; 80; 70; 50.

Assessment Activities—

    1. Cat, dog, elephant, flag.

    2. On, pear, queen, rat.

    3. 24, 56, 71.

Chapter 4
Answer Key
Page 29 – Circle the h, underline the a, draw a box around the t.

Page 30 – Circle the s, underline the u, draw a box around the n.

Page 31 – Circle the carrots, draw a box around the corn.

Page 32 – 27, 26, 25, 24, 23, 22, 21, 20, 19, 18, 17, 16, 15,
        14, 13, 12, 11, 10, 9, 8, 7, 6, 5, 4, 3, 2, 1.

Page 33 – 4, 14, 7, 2, 18.

Assessment Activities—

    1. Write the names and circle the sounds.

    2. Draw the item sets.

    3. 16, 27, 4 and 1, 16.

Chapter 5
Answer Key
Page 36 – Circle man, pan, bag, van.

Page 37 – Circle castle, bag, pan, crab.

Page 38 – Lid/yes, cup/no, bib/yes, can/no, cat/no, mat/no, fin/yes, pin/yes.

Page 39 – 4 + 2 = 6, 1 + 4 = 5, 5 + 3 = 8.

Page 40 – Color 80, 52, 26, 95, and 19.

Assessment Activities—

    1. bid, big, bin, or bit; bad, bag, ban, bar, or bat;
      did, dig, dim, or dip; dab, dad, or dam.

    2. 5, 9.

    3. 22, 40, 62, 18, 51, 88.

Answer Key

Chapter 6
Answer Key

Page 43 – Cross out ball, bat, rat, dog, box, and apple.

Page 44 – Color mop, box, fox, and sock.

Page 45 – 9 – 2 = 7, 8 – 4 = 4, 6 – 3 = 3.

Page 46 – 5, 6, 7, 8, 9, 10, 11, 12, 13, 14.

Page 47 – Color 8 + 4, 5+7, 11+1, 7+5, 10+2, 12+0, 2+10, 3+9, and 9+3.

Assessment Activities—

    1. Big, dig, fig, jig, pig, rig, wig; bop, hop, mop, pop, or top.

    2. First column: 5, 2, 2, 2.

       Second column: 8, 8, 8, 8.

Chapter 7
Answer Key

Page 50 – Circle the clock, log, frog, sock, and box.

Page 51 – Mud, rug, nut, and cup.

Page 52 – Circle the sun, rug, brush, bug, and nut.

Page 53 – 4 + 2 = 6, 3 + 1 = 4, 2 + 3 = 5.

Page 54 – 6 + 6 = 12, 5 + 5 = 10, 4 + 4 = 8, 3 + 3 = 6,

         2 + 2 = 4, 1 + 1 = 2, 0 + 0 = 0.

Assessment Activities—

    1. Add ending letters.

    2. Think of rhyming words.

    3. 4 + 3 = 7.

Chapter 8
Answer Key

Page 57 – Color pen, neck, dress, and bed.

Page 58 – Circle nest, sled, bed, and stem.

Page 59 – 2 + 3 = 5, 5 + 6 = 11, 3 + 4 = 7, 1 + 2 = 3, 4 + 5 = 9, 0 + 1 = 1.

      T E R R I F I C

Page 60 – 2 + 2 + 4 = 8,   1 + 1 + 1 + 2 = 5,   4 + 5 + 2 = 11,   3 + 3 + 3 + 3 = 12,

         2 + 1 + 4 = 7,   1 + 4 + 3 = 8,   1 + 1 + 5 = 7.

Page 61 – 1, 1, 8, 8.

Assessment Activities—

    1. Add a consonant to the end of each word.

    2. Circle 3, sum is 7. Circle 2, sum is 5. Circle 4, sum is 9. Circle 6, sum is 13.

    3. Circle 2, sum is 7. Circle 5, sum is 7. Circle 1, sum is 6. Circle 3, sum is 6.

Answer Key

Chapter 9
Answer Key

Page 64 – Color tub and bug.

Page 65 – Circle bat, fan, and Sam.

Page 66 – E, R, and A.

       G R E A (T)

Page 67 – 1 = 12¢, 2 = 26¢, 3 = 10¢, 4 = 7¢, 5=29¢.

Page 68 – Color all sections with coins red.

Assessment Activities—

    1. Circle CAT and MAT.

    2. Add the A sound to make BAND, SAND, and HAND.

    3. Answers will vary.

Chapter 10
Answer key

Page 71 – Net, ten, hen, and web.

Page 72 – "i" bag contains wig, pin, and fish.

       "o" bag contains rod, pot, and top.

Page 73 – Red groups – 10 pennies, two nickels, 1 dime, 5 pennies and 1 nickel.

       Blue groups – 3 dimes, 2 dimes and 2 nickels.

       Green groups – 2 quarters, 5 dimes.

Page 74 – 1 = 2 pennies, 2 = 3 pennies, 3 = 2 pennies, 4 = 2 pennies, 5 = 4 pennies.

Page 75 – Fill in names, amount of coins, and value of coins. Draw the coins.

Assessment Activities—

    1. TUB, BUG, RUG and BAT, HAT, CAT

    2. $0.30, $0.25, $0.40,

    3. PIG-WIG, HEN-TEN, POT-HOT

Answer Key

Chapter 11
Answer Key

Page 78 – Draw lines between net, wet, pet, and vet.

Page 79 – Kim, Tim, and Jim.

Page 80 – Cot/pot, pan/fan, lip/dip, and hen/pen.

Page 81 – 18-17, 14-13, 6-5.

Page 82 – 1. 3 - 1 = 2.

        2. 2 - 1 = 1 .

        3. 3 - 2 = 1.

Assessment Activities—

    1. 7, 9, 12, 15, 18.

    2. RING, PING, STRING.

    3. 5 – 3 = 2   6 – 2 = 4   3 – 1 = 2   4 – 1 = 3

Chapter 12
Answer Key

Page 85 – Circle fat cat, pup cup, red bed, and sad lad.

Page 86 – Dot/pot, wet/net, fan/man, and hid/lid.

Page 87 – Circle dig, wig, and jig.

Page 88 – Circle the kangaroos, 6 - 2 = 4; Circle the lions, 5 – 3 = 2; circle the seals, 6 – 3 = 3;
       circle the lions, 4 - 3 = 1.

Page 89 – 9 – 8 = 1   8 – 4 = 4

Assessment Activities—

    1. 12 – 6 = 6   4 - 2 = 2   9 – 1 = 8   10 - 8 = 2   6 – 3 = 3   11 - 7 = 4

    2. Circle: BAT/CAT, FAN/MAN, and TEN/HEN.

    3. Cat, fat, hat, mat, pat, rat, sat, or vat.

Answer Key

Chapter 13
Answer key

Page 92 – Write and draw a cat, hat, mat, rat or vat.

Page 93 – Write and draw a net, write and draw a dot or a pot, write and draw a bun, gun, nun, or the sun.

Page 94 – 1. 6 - 1 = 5

2. Circle 1 crow; 8 - 1 = 7

3. Circle 4 chickens; 11 - 4 = 7

4. Circle 4 pigs; 10 - 4 = 6

Page 95 – The subtraction problems are: the stars on the left, moons on right, flying saucers on right, planets on right, rockets on left.

Page 96 – 1/D, 2/C, 3/A,   4/E,   5/B.

Assessment Activities—

1. Circle cat and hat.

2. 12 – 2 = 10   10 – 4 = 6   1 – 1 = 0   8 – 3 = 5   5 – 0 = 5

3. 8 - 4 = 4   1 - 0 = 1   12 - 0 = 12   3 - 1 = 2   9 - 5 = 4

Chapter 14
Answer Key

Page 99 – Bat/hat, map/cap, and fat/cat.

Page 100 – Color shell and bell, color pie and eye, color king and ring.

Page 101 – B/1, C/5, D/2, E/4, A/3.

Page 102 – B/5, C/1, D/2, E/4, A/3.

Page 103 – Draw stars to describe equations.

Assessment Activities—

1. 12 - 2 = 10   3 - 0 = 3   9 - 5 = 4   7 - 6 = 1

2. Three minus zero equals three. Ten minus nine equals one. Five minus two equals three.

3. Draw pictures of the rhyming words.

Answer Key

Chapter 15
Answer Key

Page 106 – Draw a picture of each rhyming word.

Page 107 – Rug/bug, fox/box, dot/cot, and rat/mat.

Page 108 – Answers will vary.

Page 109 – Answers will vary.

Page 110 – 9 – 5 = 4, 6 + 6 = 12, 3 + 6 = 9, 9 – 2 = 7, 11 + 0 = 11, 4 + 1 = 5.

Assessment Activities—

    1. BAT, CAT, FAT, HAT, MAT, PAT, RAT, SAT.

       BET, GET, JET, LET, MET, NET, PET, SET, WET, YET.

       BIG, DIG, FIG, JIG, PIG, RIG, WIG.

    2. Answers will vary.

    3. 10 + 2 = 12   11 – 3 = 8   7 + 3 = 10   5 + 6 = 11   4 – 2 = 2   2 + 8 = 10

Chapter 16
Answer key

Page 113 – Draw lines between the bench, bridge, gate, tree, and cave.

Page 114 – Circle the words glass, map, and hat.

               Underline the words flashlight, backpack, pencil, paper, and crayon.

Page 115 – Monkey/2, kangaroo/3, pig/1, whale/1, fish/1, tiger/2.

Page 116 – 4 + 4 = 8 and 12 – 4 = 8, 12 – 3 = 9 and 6 + 3 = 9, 7 + 5 = 12 and 12 – 0 = 12.

Page 117 – 3 + 2 = 5, 5 - 2 = 3; 2 + 3 = 5, 5 – 3 = 2;

        2 + 2 = 4, 4 – 2 = 2; 2 + 2 = 4, 4 – 2 = 2.

Assessment Activities—

    1. Circle LAMP, BOOK, and LIGHT.

    2. 4 + 2 = 6   6 – 2 = 4   2 + 4 = 6   6 – 4 = 2

    3. 4 + 5 = 9   9 – 4 = 5   5 + 4 = 9   9 – 5 = 4

Answer Key

Chapter 17

Answer Key

Page 120 – Circle all the "you" words.

Page 121 – Underline all the "have" words.

Page 122 – 1. 7 + 5 = 12   2. 12 – 7 = 5   3. 5 + 7 = 12   4. 12 – 5 = 7

    5. 5 + 6 = 11   6. 11 – 5 = 6   7. 6 + 5 = 11   8. 11 – 6 = 5

Page 123 – 2. 6   3. 4   4. 5

Page 124 – 4 – 1 = 3, 2 + 4 = 6.

Assessment Activities—

1. a. 4   b. 8

2. 5 - 2 = 3   1 + 3 = 4   8 + 1 = 9   7 + 5 = 12

3. 2 + 5 = 7   5 + 2 = 7   7 – 2 = 5   7 – 5 = 2

Chapter 18

Answer key

Page 127 – Color every space with the word "go."

Page 128 – Circle the word "to" in each sentence.

Page 129 – Follow the pictures and connect them with lines.

Page 130 – Draw pictures that show addition or subtraction, such as add an egg to the nest or remove a flower from the bouquet. Then write the appropriate number sentence.

Page 131 – Circle the +, circle the +, circle the -, circle the -.

Assessment Activities—

1. Circle the +, circle the -, circle the +, circle the -.

2. 10 + 5 = 15   9 + 4 = 13   8 – 7 = 1   4 + 4 = 8

    3 – 3 = 0   16 – 1 = 15   12 + 2 = 14   5 – 2 = 3

Chapter 19

Answer Key

Page 134 – Circle the examples of "do." (There are 5.)

Page 135 – There are five examples of "said."

Page 136 – Red: Stop, Feeding Zone, Monkeys Ahead, No Littering, and Be Careful.

    Blue: Kangaroo Crossing, Tigers Live Here, No Swimming, and Quiet, Animals Sleeping.

Page 137 – 2 circles, 1 trapezoid, 3 triangles, 1 rectangle, 2 octagons, and 1 hexagon.

Assessment Activities—

2. A hexagon has 6 sides. An octagon has 8 sides.

3. Hexagon, trapezoid, triangle, square, circle, and octagon.

Answer Key

Chapter 20
Answer Key

Page 141 – Is, are, a, do.

Page 142 – Match each word on the bird with the word on the branch.

Page 143 – Match the shapes.

Page 144 – Color each section with a cube green.

Page 145 – Trace each cube in the maze.

Assessment Activities—

1. Child should draw a cube.
2. Answers will vary.
3. IS – IS
   MY – MY
   ARE – ARE
   TO – TO

Chapter 21
Answer Key

Page 148 – Circle kick, stand, and sleep.

Page 149 – Match sad, happy, and tired with the correct picture.

Page 150 – Cross out each word as you find it on the next page.

Page 151 – Circle the words found on the previous page.

Page 152 – Circle the words awake, hungry, cold, and wet.

Assessment Activities—

1. Draw a sad, happy, and mad face.
2. AWAKE, COLD, EMPTY, WET.
3. A pyramid.

Chapter 22
Answer Key

Page 155 – Underline baby, Mom, Dad, Meg, and Joe.

Page 156 – Circle teacher, doctor, sailor, pilot, and queen.

Page 157 – Draw lines to the boy, the girl, the baby, and the woman.

Page 158 – Write plant, insect, bat, and rat.

Page 159 – Trace the pyramids.

Assessment Activities—

1. Circle KING, MOM, and DAD.
2. Use the names in a sentence.
3. Draw a pyramid.

Answer Key

Chapter 23
Answer Key

Page 162 – Connect the stars starting with the number 1, then write the word "see" in each line and add the letter "f" to the last word.

Page 163 – Write the word "was" in each sentence.

Page 164 – Color 4 stop signs.

Page 165 – Color the three cubes green and the three pyramids yellow.

Page 166 – Color each triangular prism purple.

Assessment Activities—

1. A triangle and a rectangle.

2. Three rectangles and two triangles.

3. I see the dog.   I did not see.   He was happy.

Chapter 24
Answer Key

Page 169 – Underline it, did we, and i.

Page 170 – Circle "the space walk was fun." "we met Zan on a planet." and "how are you?"

Page 171 – Color each section with a green sphere.

Page 172 – Step 1: North 4 + 4 = 8; West 4 + 4 = 8, South 4, 4.

Step 2: 4 feet. 4 + 4 + 4 + 4 + 4 = 20.

Step 3: 8 + 8 + 4 = 20. 20 Horseshoes.

Page 173 – Trace each triangular prism

Assessment Activities—

1. I am happy.   We are going to the park.   Are you a frog?

2. The cat was yellow.   What is your favorite toy?   Did you go to the park?

3. 3 + 4 + 1 = 8   8 + 1 + 1 = 10   6 + 7 + 2 = 15

   5 + 1 + 2 = 8   3 + 3 + 3 = 9   4 + 1 + 2 = 7

Answer Key

Chapter 25
Answer Key

Page 176 – Circle the exclamation points at the end of the first, third, fourth, and sixth sentences.

Page 177 – Place an exclamation point at the end of each sentence and write a sentence.

Page 178 – Trace each sphere (total of 8).

Page 179 – Draw a scoop of ice cream on each cone (total of 6).

Page 180 – Color each cylinder red (total of 7).

Assessment Activities—

    1. I love you!   How are you?   I'm sleepy.   What time is it?

    2. To show emotion, excitement, or emphasis.

    3. Make a drawing of a person using a sphere, cone, and cylinder.

Chapter 26
Answer Key

Page 183 – Circle the following: We will fly in space. Sam has a space hat. I like to be in space.

Page 184 – Cross out the following: Will fly. Is big. In a spaceship. Have a spaceship.

Page 185 – Color the following stars: We are up in the sky. We can go to a star. A star is in the sky.

Page 186 – Trace the cylinders. (There are 5).

Page 187 – Yes, if he turns it on the flat side; No, too hard to stand on; No, he can't balance on it; Yes, the flat sides make it easy to stand on.

Assessment Activities—

    3. Ice cream cone, carrot

Chapter 27
Answer Key

Page 190 – Space, Star, Sky.

Page 191 – Paige is in the car. The car is red. A robot is on a rock. A hat is on the dog. The star is up in the sky.

Page 192 – I can push. We can walk!

Page 193 – The spaceship can fly in space.

Assessment Activities—

    2. Show graphic of correct answer

Answer Key

Chapter 28
Answer Key

Page 197 – I am in space. I am in the spaceship. I see the moon.

Page 198 – In; out; in; out.

Page 199 – The sky is blue. I can see the moon. The moon is big and yellow. We are out of the spaceship.

Assessment Activities—

   3. Sphere, cube, cylinder

Chapter 29
Answer Key

Page 204 – We, Is, My.

Page 205 – Walk, climb, swing.

Page 206 – Tiger, parrot, elephant.

Page 207 – Cone and sphere, cylinder and cube.

Assessment Activities—

   1. The lion ate an apple; a dog was on the planet; we were on planet Yum.

Chapter 30
Answer Key

Page 211 – Circle home, school, park, and store.

Page 212 – Underline desert, garden, beach, and school.

Page 213 – Underline boy and teacher. Circle school, library, and park.

Page 215 – Quincy is thinking about a triangular prism.

Page 216 – There are 4 pyramids, 4 cones, 4 cubes, and 4 cylinders.

Assessment Activities—

   1. Draw a circle around home.
      Draw a circle around beach.
      Draw a circle around store.

   2. The following should be underlined: teacher, friend, lifeguard.

Answer Key

Chapter 31
Answer Key

Page 219 – Draw lines to match the bat, lizard, snake, and fox.

Page 220 – Hat.

Page 221 – People: dancer, sister. Places: cave, zoo. Things: top, hat.

Page 222 – 5 rows.

Page 223 – Answers will vary.

Assessment Activities—

    1. A circle around the cave and the zoo. A line under the hat and the top.

    2. 5.

    3. 28, 47, 34.

Chapter 32
Answer Key

Page 226 – Top row: nap, jump. Bottom row: sit, draw.

Page 227 – Fish – swim, Girl – dance, Boy – run, Frog – hop.

Page 228 – Circle each pyramid.

Page 229 – Circle the horse.

Page 230 – Sam is thinking about the triangular prism.

Assessment Activities—

    1. The fish are swimming. The frog is hopping. The boy is running.

    2. Paige 1 is coloring. Paige 2 is napping. Paige 3 is walking.

Chapter 33
Answer Key

Page 233 – Circle dig, pull, draw, and ride.

Page 234 – Answers may vary.

Page 235 – Circle $\frac{1}{4}$, $\frac{1}{2}$, $\frac{1}{3}$.

Page 236 – Add the days Thursday, Friday, and Saturday. Fill in the numbers 4, 6, 8, 10, 12, and 14. 2 bananas on Sunday; 4 on Monday, and 14 on Saturday.

Page 237 – A – 4, B – 1, C – 3, D – 2.

Assessment Activities—

    1. Drawing, Digging, Pulling.

    2. 7.

Answer Key

Chapter 34
Answer Key
Page 240 – Top row: dance, kick. Bottom row: sing, swim.

Page 241 – Fish (Action words = climb, fly, swim).

Page 242 – Answers will vary.

Page 243 – A – 3, B – 2, C – 4, D – 1.

Page 244 – 16 moons.

Assessment Activities—

    1. The little boy.

    2. 11.

Chapter 35
Answer Key
Page 247 – 1. Heart, heart, diamond, oval, heart, heart.

        2. Square, hexagon, triangle, square, hexagon, triangle.

        3. 5, 6, 4.

Page 248 – Connect the dots and circle the word ride.

Page 249 – Answers will vary.

Page 250 – Circle 16. Circle girls.

Page 251 – Circle socks, stormcloud, and cornstalks.

Assessment Activities—

    1. Circle "Andrew wakes up" and underline "Andrew leaves for school."

    2. 4 carrots on Wednesday and six carrots on Thursday.

    3. Thursday.

Chapter 36
Answer Key
Page 254 – Draw a picture of a blue flower and a red flower. Draw a picture of a large frog and a small fly.

Page 255 – Circle climb, kick, ride, and run. Underline tree, ball, bike, and grass.

Page 256 – Circle walk, play, and eat. Underline baby. Draw a box around desert, and park.

Page 257 – Step: 1 draw two birds. Step 2: draw 3 birds. Step 3: draw 1 bird. Step 4: Quincy saw 6 birds.

Page 258 – Upper-right analog clock and lower-right digital clock (8:30);

        Lower-left analog clock and lower-left digital clock (4:30);

        Lower-right analog clock and upper-left digital clock (6:30).

Assessment Activities—

    1. Climb, kick, ride, run.

    2. 9.

Answer Key

Chapter 37
Answer Key

Page 261 – People: doctor, girl, boy. Places: garden, school, desert.

Page 262 – Answers will vary.

Page 263 – 5:30 Little hand on 5, big hand on 6.

2:30 Little hand on 2, big hand on 6.

11:30 Little hand on 11, big hand on 6.

7:30 Little hand on 7, big hand on 6.

3:30 Little hand on 3, big hand on 6.

Page 264 – Top: image on right has less area. Middle: image on left. Bottom: image on left.

Page 265 – From top to bottom, the corresponding numbers are 4, 3, 6, 2, 9, and 1.

Assessment Activities—

1. Rectangle 1: 2 parts; rectangle 2: 3 parts; rectangle 3: 4 parts.

2. Ride, sit, talk, read. Home, to school, on a field trip.

Chapter 38
Answer Key

Page 268 – Popcorn is spilled (right hand picture).

Page 269 – Answers will vary.

Page 270 – The boy found his dog (middle picture).

Page 271 – Bat in the middle ($\frac{1}{3}$); bat on the right side ($\frac{1}{4}$).

Page 272 – Color 1 top; color 1 kite; color 1 block.

Assessment Activities—

1. Answers will vary.

2. A. One line dividing the rectangle into 2 equal pieces. B. Rectangle is divided into 4 equal pieces with 2 or 3 lines. C. Rectangle is divided into 3 equal pieces with 2 lines.

Chapter 39
Answer Key

Page 275 – The zoo.

Page 276 – Answers will vary.

Page 278 – Paige meets Sam. They looked in the mailbox. They went to the party.

Page 279 – In the first pool, color in one section.

In the second pool, color in two sections.

In the third pool, color in three sections.

Assessment Activities—

1. A boy. Quincy. The Zookeeper. Marco.

2. The zoo.

Answer Key

Chapter 40
Answer Key

Page 283 – Paige and Sam went to a parade. Paige and Sam marched with Sally.

Page 285 – Cross out: The eagle put the sun in the sky.

Cross out: The animals went swimming.

Cross out: The moon was bright.

Page 286 – 2: Circle. 3: Heart. 4: Hexagon.

Assessment Activities—

1. They are at a parade.

2. Square, heart, heart.

Chapter 41
Answer Key

Page 289 – Circle the first sentence, star the middle sentence, and underline the last sentence.

Page 290 – The mother bird leaves her nest. She finds a worm. She feeds her baby birds.

Page 291 – 2. A, B, B, A 3. A, A, B 4. A, B, C, C 5. A, A, B, B, A, C.

Page 292 – 2. A, B, C, A, B, C 3. A, A, B, C, A, A, B, C 4. A, B, B, C, A, A, B, B, C, A.

Page 293 – 1 + 1 = 2   2 + 1 = 3   3 + 1 = 4   4 + 1 = 5   5 + 1 = 6

Assessment Activities—

1. 1, 2, 3.

2. Your child should describe the story from page 289.

3. A, B, C, C, A, B, C, C.

Chapter 42
Answer Key

Page 296 – Answers will vary.

Page 298 – Answers will vary.

Page 299 – Answers will vary.

Page 300 – Upper box is the middle, middle box is the beginning, and lower box is the end.

Assessment Activities—

1. The bird has the cheese.

2. Circle the last picture of the fox getting the cheese.

3. Answers will vary.

Answer Key

Chapter 43
Answer Key
Page 303 – An elephant has a trunk. The elephant is picking up leaves with its trunk.

Page 304 – The Three Bears are third from the top. The Gingerbread Man is at the bottom. The Frog Prince is at the top. The Princess is second from the top.

Page 305 – ... will ride his bike to the movies.

Page 306 – Answers will vary.

Page 307 – Icicles, cap, trees, and seal.

Assessment Activities—

    1. Shovel. Dig a hole.

    2. Circle at C1. Heart at B3. Square at D4.

Chapter 44
Answer Key
Page 310 – In the jungle. Lots of Animals. A tiger.

Page 310 – Spray water, pat a baby, and hug.

Page 311 – An elephant. Gray. In the jungle.

Page 312 – 1. Spray water, 2. Pat a baby, 3. hug.

Page 313 – Draw an igloo. Draw a hat.

Page 314 – 1.

Assessment Activities—

    1. At the grocery store. Oranges.

    2. At the store, Johnny and Kat see lots of fruits and vegetables. Kat wants to buy grapes.

    3. Hat, Gloves.

Chapter 45
Answer Key
Page 317 – To a store. A monkey.

Page 318 – Bananas and mangos. Answers will vary.

Page 319 – She lifted him to the leaf.

Page 320 – Mittens at position 6 and 1. Hat at position 3 and 7.

Page 321 – Trace and color the flips.

Assessment Activities—

    1. Play, sled, throw snowballs, and build a snowman.

    2. Snowman at 6.

    3. Circle the rabbits; Put an X on the boots.

Answer Key

Chapter 46
Answer Key
Page 324 – Yes, snakes do have scales. No, they do not have legs.

Page 325 – To look like a leopard. He painted spots on himself.

Page 326 – In the water. Webbed toes. They help it swim.

Page 327 – Trace and color the turns.

Page 328 – Row two, color the hat. Row three, color the bird.

Assessment Activities—

1. Yes, no, yes.
2. Answers will vary.
3. A cloud. A snowflake.

Chapter 47
Answer Key
Page 331 – Bird. Colorful. Seeds, fruits, and bugs.

Page 332 – A big cat. A cub. Swim and climb trees.

Page 333 – It has red eyes. It likes a wet home. They sleep in the day.

Page 334 – Up. Left. Down. Right. Up. Yellow.

Page 335 – Top row: Jimmy and Derek. Middle row: Suzanne, Jose, and Claude. Bottom row: Janet and Maria.

Assessment Activities—

1. Sounds they hear.
2. Stripes. Claws. Teeth.
3. Jimmy and Derek.

Chapter 48
Answer Key
Page 339 – The eggs hatch into tadpoles. Tadpoles grow arms and legs.

Page 340 – Jen, Meg, and Max. A playground.

Page 341 – Circle Joe.

Page 342 – Draw a snowman on the left side of the pole marker. Draw a penguin to the right of Marco. Draw an igloo behind the penguin. Draw icicles above the pole marker.

Assessment Activities—

1. Max, Jen, Meg, and mom. The dining room.
2. Marge's snowman is to the left of Joe's. It is under Clark's and above Kit's.

Answer Key

Chapter 49

Answer Key

Page 345 – 2, 4, 6, 8, 10, 12, 14, 16, 18, 20.

  8
  8,10
  10,12
  12,14
  14,16
  16,18
  18,20

Page 346 – Top to bottom: 3, 2, 1.

Page 347 – Circle 2.

Page 348 – Circle the middle set of shoes.

Page 349 – Scarf – turn (blue). Boots – flip (red). Sled – slide (green).

Assessment Activities—

   1. Julius woke up.

   2. Circle the sled. Place an X on the boots. Draw a line under the scarf.

   3. Cross out "Judy will go to her room," and "Judy will eat dinner."

Chapter 50

Answer Key

Page 352 – Top row: 1, 2. Bottom row: 4, 3.

Page 354 – Top row: 2, 4. Bottom row: 1, 3.

Page 355 – 1. Mittens.

   2. Hat.

   3. Boots.

Assessment Activities—

   1. ...to places they could eat grass.

Teacher Biography

Brighter Minds Publishing is committed to creating books for children that provide fun and valuable learning experiences. Highly qualified educators guided the selection of content used in the **30-Minute-A-Day Learning System Workbooks**. They are:

Jodi Lee

Jodi has undergraduate degrees in both Art Education and Communication Disorders, and a Master's degree in Elementary Education. Her classroom experience ranges from Kindergarten to Fourth Grade. Currently, she teaches Kindergarten classes at The Wellington School (Columbus, Ohio) with additional responsibilities for developing new, age-appropriate curriculum for the school's youngest students.

Leigh Anne Easterling

Leigh Anne developed the Kindergarten program for the Mary Evans Child Development Center in Columbus, Ohio where she currently teaches. Her undergraduate degree in in Early Childhood Development and she is certified in Elementary Education. In 2005, Leigh Anne was named Teacher of the Year for the State of Ohio by the National Association for the Education of Young Children.

Martha Swanson

Martha has a Bachelor of Science in Finance degree and worked for a number of years at the Highlights for Children, Inc. business office before embarking on a career in education. For the past seven years, she has taught Pre-Kindergarten for the Holy Trinity Child Development Program (Columbus, OH), an accredited member of the National Academy of Early Childhood Programs.

Sarah Raines

Sarah has a Bachelor's degree in Reading, a Master's in Educating Gifted Children, and a Doctorate of Education in Administration. She has seven years experience as a classroom teacher and five years as a school administrator. Sarah is Head of the Lower School, including pre-Kindergarten through Fourth Grade, at The Wellington School in Columbus, Ohio. She leads an ongoing initiative to develop effective, engaging curriculum for young students.

A B C D E F G H I J

K L M N O P Q R S

T U V W X Y Z

use these pages to practice writing letters and numbers

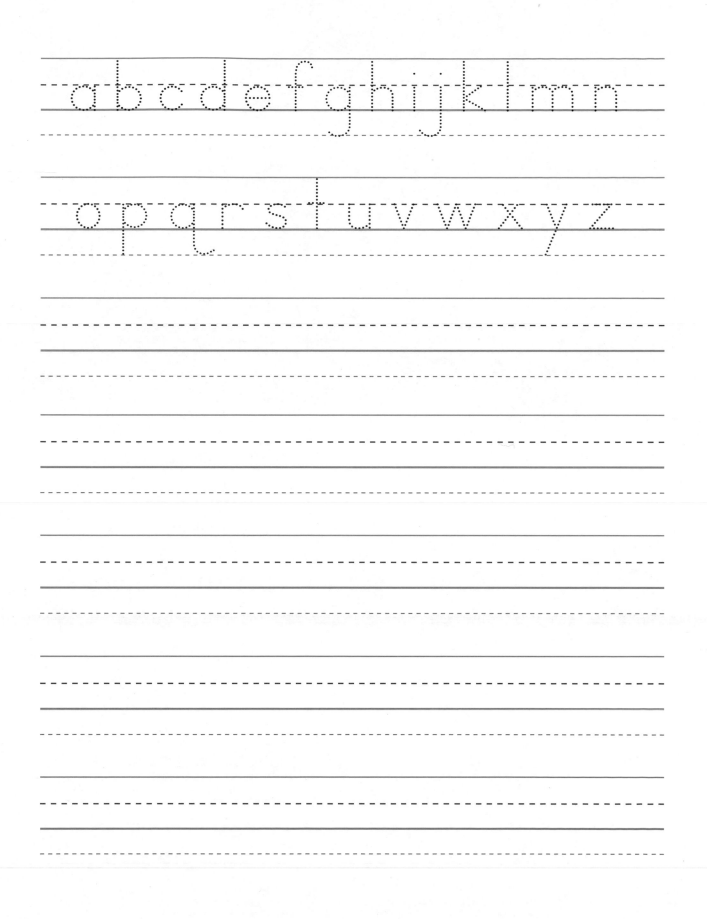

use these pages to practice writing letters and numbers

My name is

use these pages to practice writing letters and numbers

use these pages to practice writing letters and numbers

I am _____ years old.

use these pages to practice writing letters and numbers

use these pages to practice writing letters and numbers

use these pages to practice writing letters and numbers

use these pages to practice writing letters and numbers

This page has been provided for use with the assessment pages at the end of each chapter.

This page has been provided for use with the assessment pages at the end of each chapter.

This page has been provided for use with the assessment pages at the end of each chapter.

This page has been provided for use with the assessment pages at the end of each chapter.

This page has been provided for use with the assessment pages at the end of each chapter.

This page has been provided for use with the assessment pages at the end of each chapter.

This page has been provided for use with the assessment pages at the end of each chapter.

This page has been provided for use with the assessment pages at the end of each chapter.